EARTHLIGHT

poems by

ANDRÉ BRETON

Translated from the French
with an introduction and notes

by Bill Zavatsky and Zack Rogow

BLACK WIDOW PRESS

Boston, MA

EARTHLIGHT

Clair de terre

Earthlight

Some of these poems have previously appeared in *SUN, The American Poetry Review, Antaeus, The Paris Review,* and *André Breton: Selections* (University of California Press).

These translations are based on the text *Clair de terre* by André Breton published in 1966 by Éditions Gallimard in its NRF Collection Poésie.

Black Widow Press is an imprint of Commonwealth Books, Inc., Boston, MA. Distributed to the trade by NBN (National Book Network) throughout North America, Canada, and the U.K. All Black Widow Press books are printed on acid-free paper, and glued into bindings. Black Widow Press and its logo are registered trademarks of Commonwealth Books, Inc.

Joseph S. Phillips and Susan J. Wood, Ph.D., Publishers
www.blackwidowpress.com

Cover Art:
André Breton, b. 1896, Tinchebray, France – 1966, Paris
Self Portrait: Automatic Writing, 1930
Photocollage, 26.5 x 23.5 cm
The Vera and Arturo Schwarz Collection of Dada and Surrealist Art in the Israel Museum
© ADAGP, Paris
Accession number: B03.0149

Design & production: Kerrie Kemperman

ISBN-13: 978-0-9960079-3-1

Printed in the United States
10 9 8 7 6 5 4 3 2 1

CONTENTS

MONT DE PIÉTÉ / PAWNSHOP (1919)

CLAIR DE TERRE / EARTHLIGHT (1923)

L'UNION LIBRE / FREE UNION (1931)

LE REVOLVER A CHEVEUX BLANCS / THE REVOLVER WITH WHITE HAIR (1932)

VIOLETTE NOZIÈRES / VIOLETTE NOZIERES (1933)

L'AIR DE L'EAU / THE AIR OF THE WATER (1934)

AU LAVOIR NOIR / IN THE BLACK LAUNDRY SHED (1936)

TRANSLATOR'S INTRODUCTION

by Bill Zavatsky

Beginning in 1988, and for the next twenty years, Éditions Gallimard published four volumes of André Breton's complete works in the Bibliothèque de la Pléiade series, the last—Breton's writings on art—in 2008. The editions are beautifully produced, fully annotated, and quite expensive. From April to August of 1991 an exhibition at the Centre Pompidou in Paris entitled "Beauty Will Be Convulsive" (the penultimate words of *Nadja*) memorialized Breton's life-long activity as a tastemaker in the arts. Then in 1995 Mark Polizzotti's masterful biography, *Revolution of the Mind: The Life of André Breton,* appeared. From February to May of 2002, the Metropolitan Museum of Art in New York City presented a huge exhibition called "Surrealism: Desire Unbound." In addition, important first translations of major works by Breton—including *Mad Love* (1987) and *Communicating Vessels* (1990)—appeared during those years. Zack Rogow's translation of *Arcanum 17* came out as well, in 1994. Another irony came in the spring of 2003, when the poet's vast personal collection of artworks, manuscripts, and books was dispersed at auction to an international outcry. (Many felt that it should have remained in

France.) Perhaps this dissemination of the body and soul of André Breton indicates once and for all that he and his work and surrealism itself have entered the public domain.

Which is to say that André Breton, ironically for years one of the least translated members of the surrealist movement that he engineered and directed, has now become its most in-print-in-English figure, and some brief note ought to be taken especially of the translations of his poetry that have appeared in our language.

Breton's writing began to appear in English translation in American—or, more accurately—expatriate literary journals from the 1920s on. What is surprising, however, is how few of his poems were translated; primarily he was presented as the polemicist-spokesman of surrealism. There is poetry of his in the famous 1932 "Surrealist Number" of *This Quarter,* and work appeared in the 200-page-plus "Surrealist Section" of *New Directions 1940*. But *VVV,* an American surrealist magazine published in New York during World War II, and of which Breton was an editor, brought out his poetry without benefit of translation. It was not until 1946, through Charles Henri Ford's View Editions, an offshoot of his surrealist-influenced *View* magazine, that Breton came to have an entire book to himself in English, albeit it a tiny one (twenty-five pages of translated text). Its name was *Young Cherry Trees Secured Against Hares [Jeunes cerisiers guarantis contre les lièvres],* translated by Edouard Roditi, with drawings by Arshile Gorky.

The funny look-through cover by Marcel Duchamp replaced the face of the Statue of Liberty with the austere visage of Breton himself.

Young Cherry Trees Secured Against Hares contained eleven poems, two of them excerpts, with the French texts published *en face*. Included were a few of Breton's most famous works, among them "Au regard des divinités," "Tournesol," and "L'Union libre." The real problem with the book is Roditi's language, which has energy but doesn't sound like American English. Reading it is like watching all those movies, Hollywood films included, in which foreigners are made to speak with a British accent. Or to say it better, perhaps, the poems are cast in the meta-language that is part French, part English, and totally fishy. I and my collaborator, who write poetry in the American language, assumed from the very beginning that the Breton we would attempt to bring into English should resonate with the language of Walt Whitman and Allen Ginsberg. If it sounds presumptuous, the fact is that the very process of translation ensures that Breton will no longer sound like a Frenchman.

To an extent we experienced the same difficulties reading Kenneth White's very good and often inspiring 1967 selection of Breton translations. Breton was still talking like James Mason in some of them. When in 1974 David Antin's versions of four Breton poems appeared in Michael Benedikt's anthology *The Poetry of Surrealism*, however, we perked up. Here

was an *American* poet's voice "doing" Breton—a voice that we could learn something from. There was no "method" of Antin's to adopt, but the important example of making it swift and uncluttered has served us as one kind of model in our translation effort. Mary Ann Caws's and Jean-Pierre Cauvin's *Poems of André Breton* appeared in 1982, well after we had begun our work, but it furnished us with another kind of model, that of rigorous scholarship as we came to grips intellectually with these often impenetrable poems.

Why hasn't Breton's poetry received the translation attention that it seems to merit, if only by virtue of his position as leader of the surrealist movement? (We might just as well ask, of course, why surrealist poetry in general has been so poorly and so little translated, or even proceed directly to the Big Question: why poetry itself gets such minuscule slices of the publishing and reviewing pies). Sticking to Breton, one answer may be that most of the attention attracted by surrealism was due to its fine art productions. Even teenagers recognize the René Magritte paintings that regularly appear as the cover art of popular recordings; everybody has had a laugh over Dalí's "floppy watches." Indeed, so much brilliant work in all media was produced by surrealist artists that the poetry of the movement might well go unnoticed, or find itself crushed under the weight of so much visual genius. You don't have to know much (or any) French to appreciate the collages of Max Ernst, nor do you have to "translate" anything to take in the images of surrealist films. That the artwork has also come to be worth

enormous sums of money also creates a perspective on the poetry, especially given the financial returns that a translator can expect from his or her labors.

The politics of personality in which Breton was enmeshed also seems to have had repercussions for his career as a translated poet. The likeliest candidate to have brought out a collection of Breton's poetry was James Laughlin of New Directions, who published many of Breton's cohorts (including a volume of Paul Éluard's selected poems) in the New Directions annual anthologies that began to appear in 1936. While it is true that Breton's long poem *Fata Morgana* had a prominent place in the 1941 annual, Laughlin—who had been introduced to Éluard and Breton by a contributor to his anthologies—later told a reporter from the *New York Times Book Review* that he had liked Éluard's "simple straightforwardness... so much in contrast to the deviousness or exhibitionism of some others of the Surrealist Group." Laughlin also said that he had "never cared for" Breton's work as much, which might clarify the identity of at least one of the surrealists that he disliked (*NYTBR*, 25 February 1973, 13).

Another literary-political consideration. The fact might have rankled that the Magus of Surrealism never quite came to grips with the United States, his host country, during his stint as a Voice of America announcer in New York City. (*VVV*, for example, published most of its best work in French.) Americans haven't much cottoned to the idea of literary schools, either—neither the Imagist group of 1907, ruthlessly parodied

as the "Spectric School" by Witter Bynner and Arthur Davison Ficke in 1916; nor the (for a time) feared and insulted New York School, proud of its Francophile tendencies, composed of Frank O'Hara, John Ashbery, Kenneth Koch, and James Schuyler. The idea of "school" or "group" has struck most literary Americans, rightly or wrongly, as too European; that is, too old-country and a mite too communistic to countenance our tradition of rugged individualism. Americans think that there should not be rules for literary composition; that by virtue of collectivity one should not attain a more advantageous position than anyone else; that art cannot be manufactured by committee.

Then there was the Breton of the imperious gaze, who always looked as if he were glaring from his photographs, or posing, Napoleon-like. Not for nothing was the title "The Pope of Surrealism" slapped on him. The famous (or infamous) expulsions from the surrealist group for unidealistic behavior (Robert Desnos was dumped for making a living as a journalist) were announced publicly in Breton's own manifestoes, then garnered more publicity when his former allies counterattacked. There was the bitter and very public flirtation with the Communist Party. It is no wonder that many must have come to think of him as an unpleasant man. And Breton often seemed to be "striking a pose," a pose (or a variety of them) also present in the poetry, the sense of an extremely disciplined and deeply *rational* man who is knocking himself out to have *visions.* (Perhaps they who are least likely to have visions are most in need of them.) Nevertheless, for all his modernity there

is more than a little of the nineteenth-century man in Breton, who was born in 1896, with his carefully planned hallucinations. (And such conduct is typical of most French literary hallucinators; *vide* Rimbaud's famous letters on the subject.)

The sometimes pretentious and contorted rhetoric of Breton's poems and prose can produce tormented, tangled lines and sentences that are half schoolboy imitation of Cicero and half homage to Lautréamont (himself afflicted with the taste for the periodic). The straining after farfetched metaphors does not always lift Breton's poetry into the air. Indeed, the great stumbling block to the appreciation of this work is its obscurity. (Would that we were talking of mere difficulty here!) While it is often possible to "ride the rapids" of the thought-flow of the later poems and to derive tremendous pleasure in the delight to be experienced in watching Breton's images river into an extraordinary power or disappear in a dazzle of spray-smash, his early cubist-inspired poetry presents tremendous obstacles to understanding, unless of course one is not concerned with meaning. It is perfectly possible to throw one's brains away and float upon the surface of Breton's work, but anyone who has ever attempted to translate a poem knows that a translation also delivers a reading of a poem. For better or for worse, the translator must interpret what he or she finds, and attempt to see some coherence in the whole. Or at the very least, to simply figure out what is going on. In translating many of these poems, I and my collaborator have been hard put to find the thread in the maze of images, though the information that we have dug up on the poems (a good deal of it from the

first two volumes of Breton's *Oeuvres complètes*) suggests allusions and patterns that we could never have guessed. This is where translation and scholarship join hands, but I must for my own part confess that the extent to which Breton's method of composition—his *mind,* I suppose—offers itself up to PhD candidates for further research has left me more than daunted. For an adventure that sought to shake off the shackles of the rational mind, surrealism (or at least Breton's surrealism) seems destined to have surrendered itself to parliaments of professors. There is simply no way to "get" a good deal of this poetry without the copious notes that come out of hours of hard research, and even then one is sometimes not sure what to make of it all.

"Poetry will be made by everyone." Wasn't that a Surrealist byword, one of the bedrock propositions of a movement that would restore poetry to the people and pass out the keys to the kingdom of the Marvelous in the street? Not if you read Breton. The average poetry reader, if there are any of them left (and if they ever indeed existed) won't get through this work easily, if at all. Was surrealism strictly for the brotherhood (since, despite its idealization of woman, its relationship to sisterhood seems to have been a thorny one)? The surrealists were the first poets to write under the inspiration of psychoanalysis, and free association took them directly into the personal unconscious. Pierre Reverdy, from whom Breton derived many of his ideas about metaphor, the beating heart of Surrealism, wrote: "The dream is a tunnel that runs beneath reality. It's a sewer of clear water, but it's still a sewer" ("Le rêve est un tun-

nel qui passe sous la realité. C'est un égout d'eau claire, mais c'est un égout," Reverdy, *Le Gant de crin,* 23). I don't know how comfortable I am with the word "sewer" here, but there is a common denominator in surrealist imagery (visual as well as verbal) that often makes one think the same poet has written every surrealist poem. In a collective enterprise this might not seem surprising; but on a journey into the unknown it can stultify. However, surrealism itself was rife with battles over the value of collective as opposed to individual behavior; let's leave the contradiction standing as mark in time, since there's nothing we can do to change it. From the beginning of the Movement, Breton seemed to sense that he was in search of something larger than the personal, perhaps what Jung had called the Collective Unconscious. Before we can say a word about this, though, we owe it to Breton to figure out why the two of us spent several years of our lives translating these poems if one of us has so many reservations about them.

What struck me initially about Breton's poetry, and what remains one of its great glories, is the gorgeous, often wild, often unexpected images that animate it. We have no idea where the most powerful of them are coming from, or where they are going (except deep into our own hearts and minds), and what they are going to couple with to create metaphors—connections—as compelling as any poet has ever made. As poets, I know that I can also speak for my collaborator when I say that Breton urges you to trust your own impulses when you write. The objective is a kind of pure poetry born out of the real beauty of perception twinned with originality of

metaphor—true "invention." In the best of these poems, there is nothing more exciting than watching Breton follow his mind, his heart, and his pen, fused as they have become into a single expressive instrument. Let the scholars argue about how much Breton revised his automatic texts, one gets the *feeling* that these works are being created on the spot—wham, zing, yippee!—without agony, without intervention, and with a sense of utter adventure that is rare in poetry—or in life itself. I love their fluidity, the simplicity (as in the "Five Dreams") and attention to detail that they can attain, even the philosophical grandeur-in-miniature of "Once Upon a Time to Come," in which the essay becomes a kind of prose poem. The grand statement of surrealism was that right here, right now, in this world, perhaps during a walk down the street and a chance look in the window of the local drugstore, you could find an entryway to the *other* world—the world *above* or *beyond* or *superimposed upon* this world: the lost paradise that Breton and his *confrères* searched for relentlessly like mad alchemists or exiled angels, often at great personal cost. If you could actually find this world down the street and around the corner, and the surrealists thought that it *could* be found, why then you yourself could *create* it. This is an extraordinarily empowering concept, one that all poets—all human beings—would do well to come to terms with.

Breton finds his own greatest power and is particularly communicative in his poetry most notably when his images have been generated or focused or alchemized by the power of love in masterpieces like "Free Union." The ecstatic mapping

of the lover's body by metaphor, a technique as old as poetry itself, helped to renew this form (and the idea behind it) for our century. For me perhaps the greatest work in this collection is "The Air of the Water," a sequence of love poems that never fails to thrill by its ingenuity of image and the clarity of its passionate utterance. In a poem like "Violette Nozières," though the love is objectified (it is Violette's), it is through her excessive passion that Breton can find a sociopolitical focus: What happens when desire is thwarted? How many poems like this have poets given us since the end of the Vietnam War? "Violette Nozières" can still provide a model for the poem of political action. And in rooting it in a real event, the efficaciousness of surrealist poetry comes alive.*

Metaphor-making, the dynamic principle that motivated Surrealism, asserts that all is connected, even if we must puzzle at it through a glass darkly. With the metaphor as its instrument of transformation, surrealism was another of the twentieth century's expeditions into the spirit—a grail quest for the ecstasy of the Garden of Eden, a return to the wholeness smashed to bits by the Great War in which many of the surrealists had participated. Breton's entanglement in the imagery of his own personal unconscious mirrored the greater surrealist failure to break through to the archetypal. Indeed, as far back

* "The truth of what happened in that small apartment on the top floor of 9 Rue de Madagascar in the years, months, and hours leading up to the evening of August 21, 1933, now lies deep in the soil of central France, in the cemetery of Neuvy-sur-Loire, where Violette lies buried alongside her husband, her mother, and her father." (Maza, *Violette Nozière,* 277).

as his narrative *Nadja* (1928) Breton had asked the greatest, the only question: "Who am I?" But without a center, and even with as powerful an ego as Breton's for a compass, all of the women like Nadja who mysteriously come and go in the pages of surrealism do just that—come and go—in shadowy imitation of Dante's encounter with Beatrice. Dante knew that *anima,* a dynamic of the spirit, led to the Presence that created the music of the spheres. Nadja leads Breton to the door of the insane asylum, and to the (supposedly despised) act of "making literature."

Others carrying out investigations similar in nature to those of the surrealists knew better. One of them was René Daumal, whose "Open Letter to André Breton" of 1930 (quoted here in Mark Polizzotti's translation) attacked surrealist "party games" and still offers the most nail-on-the-head criticism of Breton (and hence surrealism):

> And in the area of positive research, what have you done since the founding of Surrealism? ...We have, in answer to your *amusing science,* the study of all the processes of depersonalization, of telepathy, of clairvoyance, of mediumism; we have the unlimited field (in every conceivable mental direction) of Hindu yoga, the systematic confrontation of the lyrical and dreamlike fact with the teachings of occult tradition... and we're not finished yet. (Daumal, *The Powers of the Word,* 53)

Breton's utter aversion to anything that smacked of formal religion constituted his Achilles heel. Even a friend and sometime disciple like Octavio Paz noted that Breton's "opposition to Christianity was religious in character" (Paz, *On Poets and Others,* 68). Roger Shattuck, whose writings on surrealism are among the most enlightening, noted that "The most perceptive French critics (especially Monnerot, Carrouges, and Audoin) have insisted on the commitment of Surrealism to the spiritual and the sacred": "Occultism, objective chance, the revival of the chivalric and Arthurian traditions of erotic love, magic, and alchemy, the cult of the supernatural in woman—all these unstable items fed a faith that had unmistakable elements of transcendence" (Shattuck, *The Innocent Eye,* 43–44).

Perhaps in this "New Age" of spiritual investigation, surrealism will begin to be examined for what it increasingly seems to have been—a series of desperate and noble attempts to assuage the hunger for whatever we want to call the One that connects everything. Work has already been done, is just beginning to appear, and will be coming for years that explores Breton's involvement with alchemy and the occult.

•

This translation came about because, in best surrealist fashion, Zack Rogow and I discovered quite by accident that we were both translating Breton. Zack sent some very good translations to *SUN,* a magazine that I edited and published for a time. I was angry and envied how good his translations were,

and since I couldn't beat him, I hoped that I could join him: Why not translate Breton together? As poets who had discovered the French surrealism that in varying degrees nurtured our early work and still continues to inspire us, we wanted to see how André Breton, the leader of the movement, the eye at the center of the hurricane, sounded in the American language. Like all poets who translate, we wanted to see if Breton's work could be of use to us in our own writing. Two heads are better than one, and that four-eyed idea appealed to us. Also, translators have a nasty habit of imagining that they "own" the poet that they are working on. We thought it both good for our egos and in the spirit of surrealism to work at forgetting who had contributed what. Our work was a total collaboration. Beyond the hundreds of hours that we spent going over every word in these poems, trying to make them as accurate as we could and trying also to make them sing, we brought our versions to poet-friends and scholars whose advice and assistance has proved essential.

With this edition of *Earthlight,* our publishers Joseph Phillips and Susan Wood have allowed us to realize one of the desires that we had nurtured from the beginning—that the French text of *Clair de terre* be a part of our book. (Rights questions have prevented this until now.) Our book is a complete translation of the 1966 anthology of André Breton's poetry called *Earthlight (Clair de terre)* edited by Alain Jouffroy and published by Éditions Gallimard in the *Poésie* series.

(A subsequent anthology from the same publisher, *Signe ascendant,* selected poems from the second half of Breton's career.) This selection should not be confused with Breton's 1923 collection of poetry called *Clair de terre,* which contains poems that were omitted from the Jouffroy edition and that have not been translated here.

We owe debts of gratitude to the following individuals who read our manuscript in whole or in part and offered criticism of it: the late LeRoy C. Breunig, Emeritus Professor of French at Barnard College and Columbia University; Adelaide Russo, Associate Professor of French at Louisiana State University (Baton Rouge); Ron Padgett, poet and translator; the late Anna Balakian, Emerita Professor of French and Comparative Literature at New York University; and Serge Gavronsky, poet, novelist, translator, critic, and Professor Emeritus of French at Barnard College. We are also grateful to Mary Ann Caws, Distinguished Professor of French, English, and Comparative Literature at the Graduate Center of the City University of New York, and Jean-Pierre Cauvin, Professor Emeritus, Department of French and Italian at the University of Texas (Austin), for a number of kindnesses that they showed us. Heartfelt thanks are also extended to Susan Bluttman, Phyllis Zavatsky, and (in memory) Anne Sachs. We would also like to thank Kerrie Kemperman for her terrific work on the design of the book and Pauline Bernard for her excellent eye in proofing the scans of the French text.

Thanks are also due to special friends of this translation, Mark Polizzotti, author of *Revolution of the Mind,* the biography of André Breton; and Laurence Lang, translator and teacher of French and Spanish at the Trinity School (New York City).

Translation is a collaborative process that can join workers of different ages, from different generations, even those of different centuries. We have read the versions done by our predecessors and have tried to learn from them as we evolved our own vision of how Breton's poetry ought to look and sound in our moment and in our language. In another decade or two we expect that another translator (or two) will come along with a more daring, more incisive vision of how Breton's poems ought to be brought into English.

MONT DE PIÉTÉ

(1919)

PAWNSHOP

(1919)

FAÇON

L’attachement vous sème en taffetas
broché projets,
sauf où le chatoiement d’ors se complut.
Que juillet, témoin fou, ne compte le péché
d’au moins ce vieux roman de fillettes qu’on lut!

De fillettes qu’on
brigua
se mouille (Ans, store au point d’oubli), faillant
téter le doux gave,
— Autre volupté quel acte élu t’instaure? —
un avenir, éclatante Cour Batave.

Étiquetant
baume vain l’amour, est-on nanti
de froideur
un fond, plus que d’heures mais, de mois? Elles
font de batiste : A jamais! — L’odeur anéantit
tout de même jaloux ce printemps,

Mesdemoiselles

WAY

Fondness strews you with brocaded
taffeta plans,
except where the sheen of gold found its delight.
Let July, mad
witness, at least count the sin
of that old novel for little girls that we read!
With little girls we
courted
dampens (Years, window blinds on the brink of oblivion), failing
to nurse at the sweet torrent,
—Further pleasure what chosen deed initiates you?—
a future, a dazzling Batavian Court.
Labeling
balm vain love, have we guaranteed
by our coldness
a foundation, more than hours but, months? The girls
Are making batiste: Forever!—Anyway the smell annihilates
this jealous spring,
Dear young ladies.

AGE

Aube, adieu! Je sors du bois hanté; j'affronte les routes, croix torrides. Un feuillage bénissant me perd. L'août est sans brèches comme une meule.

Retiens la vue panoramique, hume l'espace et dévide machinalement les fumées.

Je vais m'élire une enceinte précaire : on enjambera s'il faut le buis. La province aux bégonias chauffés caquète, range. Que gentiment s'ameutent les griffons au volant frisé des jupes!

Où la chercher, depuis les fontaines? A tort je me fie à son collier de bulles...

Yeux devant les pois de senteur.

*

Chemises caillées sur la chaise. Un chapeau de soie inaugure de reflets ma poursuite. Homme... Une glace te venge et vaincu me traite en habit ôté. L'instant revient patiner la chair.

Maisons, je m'affranchis de parois sèches. On secoue! Un lit tendre est plaisanté de couronnes.

Atteins la poésie accablante des paliers.

19 février 1916.

AGE

Dawn, farewell! I'm coming out of the haunted forest; I'm braving the roads, torrid crosses. A foliage that gives blessings is ruining me. August, like a millstone, has no cracks.

Keep the panoramic view, inhale space, and mechanically unwind coils of smoke.

I'm going to choose myself a precarious enclosure: if we need to, we'll step over the boxwood. The province with heated begonias chatters, tidies up. How nicely griffons band together on the wavy flounces of skirts!

Where to look for it, since the fountains? I'm wrong to trust its bubble necklace....

Eyes in front of the sweet peas.

*

Congealed shirts on the chair. A silk hat with reflections. Man.... A mirror avenges you and treats me, the conquered one, like a stripped-off uniform. The moment returns to paw my flesh.

Houses, I'm breaking free of parched walls. We're shaking it off! A tender bed is teased about crowns.

Achieve the overwhelming poetry of staircase landings.

February 19, 1916.

COQS DE BRUYÈRE

Coqs de bruyère… et seront-ce coquetteries
de péril
ou de casques couleur de quetsche?
Oh! surtout
qu'elle fripe un gant de suède chaud
soutenant quels
feux de Bengale gâteries!

Au Tyrol, quand les bois se foncent, de tout
l'être abdiquant un
destin
digne, au plus, de chromos savoureux,
mon
remords : sa rudesse, des maux,
je dégage les capucines de sa lettre.

GROUSE

Grouse... and will these gross coquetries be
dangerous
or helmets the color of quetsch?
Oh! above all
may it crush a warm suede glove
sustaining what
treats of Bengal lights!

In the Tyrol, when the forests darken, abdicating
with its whole being a
destiny
worthy, at least, of racy chromos,
my
remorse: her harshness, the pains,
You can smell the scent of her letters' nasturtiums on me.

ANDRÉ DERAIN

chante — pinsons — dressoir et pots crus en poète.
Il s'entend de patine à velouter;
le soir
une fleur des genêts sa corne vous lutine.
Allons !
tant qu'un neigeux Olympe déjeunait
en voulut-il
à son éclat? — Pommiers. —
                                        Songeuse
mystique aux mains
ces langes bleus comme un glaçon,
l'humain frémisse
et toi : le premier-né c'est l'ange!

— A vol d'oiseau. — Que mousse
entre vos feuilles, toits exquis,
la rose blanche et qui fond, de fumée !
Où, selon que mes doigts
débouchent à l'odeur — Mai ! — ce tube ou
d'almée
un pantalon chiffonnent,
m'épandre aussi verdeur à travers?

sings—finches—dresser and unfired poet-shaped pots.
He knows how to give something a soft patina;
evening
a flower of the brooms its spur teases you.
Oh come on!
as long as a snowy Olympus was having lunch
did he want any
when it thundered?—Apple trees.—
                                        Mystical dreaming
woman with the hands
these baby clothes blue as an icicle
May the human quiver
and you: the first-born's the angel!

—As the crow flies. —Which foams
between your leaves, exquisite roofs,
the white rose, and it melts, from the smoke!

Where, depending on whether my fingers
clear the smell from—May!—this tube or
rumple
an almah's pants,
spread greenness to me, too, through it?

Qu'un semblant de cornette bouffonne
(et ta coiffe empesée)
appelle : tout tremblant
le ramage turquin, ma sœur, des noms en zée.

Ah ! plus ce brouillard tendre.

May a semblance of burlesque cornette
(and your starched coif)
call: trembling all over
the teal floral pattern, my sister, some names ending in zee.

Ah! No more of this tender fog.

FORÊT-NOIRE*

Out

Tendre capsule etc. melon
Madame de Saint-Gobain trouve le temps long seule
Une côtelette se fane

Relief du sort
Où sans volets ce pignon blanc
Cascades
Les schlitteurs sont favorisés
Ça souffle
Que salubre est le vent le vent des crémeries

L'auteur de l'Auberge de l'Ange Gardien
L'an dernier est tout de même mort
A propos

De Tubingue à ma rencontre
Se portent les jeunes Kepler Hegel
Et le bon camarade

* *RIMBAUD PARLE*

BLACK FOREST*

Out

Tender capsule etc. derby
Madame de Saint-Gobain finds time goes by slowly when alone
A cutlet wilts
Outline of fate
Where shutterless this white gable
Waterfalls
Log-haulers are favored

It's blowing
What a wholesome wind the wind from the dairies

The author of The Guardian Angel Inn
Died last year anyhow
By the way

From Tübingen to meet me
Come young Kepler Hegel
And the faithful friend

* *RIMBAUD SPEAKING.*

POUR LAFCADIO

L'avenue   en même temps   le Gulf Stream
MAM VIVier

Ma maîtresse
prend en bonne part
son diminutif Les amis
sont à l'aise
On s'entend

Greffier
parlez M A langue M Aternelle
Quel ennui l'heure du cher corps
corps accort
Jamais je ne gagnerai tant de guerres

Des combattants
qu'importe mes vers le lent train
l'entrain
Mieux vaut laisser dire
qu'André Breton
receveur de Contributions Indirectes
s'adonne au collage
en attendant la retraite

FOR LAFCADIO

The avenue   at the same time   the Gulf Stream
MAM FISHfarm

My mistress
takes her nickname
good-naturedly Our friends
are comfortable
                    We get along
    Court clerk
speak MA MA*ternal tongue*
    what a bore the hour of the dear body
charming body
    I'll never win that many wars

Some combatants
what difference do my verses make the slow locomotion
lo! commotion
Better to let them say
that André Breton
collector of Excise Taxes
has taken up collage
while he waits for a chance to retire

MONSIEUR V

A Paul Valéry

A la place de l'étoile
L'Arc de Triomphe
qui ne ressemble à un aimant que pour la forme
argenterai-je
les jardins suspendus

BERCEUSE
L'enfant à la capote de rubans
L'enfant que chatouille la mer

En grandissant
il se regarde dans une coquille nacrée
l'iris de son œil est l'étoile
dont je parlais

MARCHE
Pierre ou Paul

Il s'apprête à tirer les rois
aujourd'hui comme ailleurs
ses égaux
Rêve de révolutions

On ne saurait décrire en art
L'engin à prendre le renard bleu

MISTER V

To Paul Valéry

In place of l'étoile
The Arc de Triomphe
which only looks like a magnet because of its amorous shape
shall I silver
the hanging gardens

LULLABY
The child with the ribbon bonnet
The child that the sea tickles.

Growing up
he looks at himself in a pearly shell
the iris of his eye is the star
I was talking about

MARCH
Peter or Paul

He gets ready to play find the king
today as elsewhere
his equals
Dreams of revolutions

It's impossible for art to depict
The device that can catch the blue fox

UNE MAISON PEU SOLIDE

Le gardien des travaux
est victime de son dévouement

Depuis longtemps le mode de construction d'un immeuble situé rue des Martyrs était jugé déraisonnable par les gens du quartier. Rien n'apparaissait encore de la toiture que déjà les peintres et les tapissiers entreprenaient de décorer les appartements. De nouveaux échafaudages étayaient tous les jours la façade chancelante, au grand trouble des passants que le gardien des travaux rassurait. Hélas! celui-ci devait payer son optimisme de la vie puisqu'hier, à midi trente, alors que les ouvriers étaient allés déjeu-ner, la bâtisse s'effondrait, l'ensevelissant sous ses décombres.

Un enfant, trouvé évanoui sur les lieux du sinistre, ne fut pas long à reprendre connaissance. C'est le jeune Lespoir, 7 ans, que l'on reconduisit bien vite à ses parents. Il avait eu plus de peur que de mal. Il commença par réclamer la *trottinette* sur laquelle il s'était élancé du haut de la rue. Le garçonnet raconte qu'un homme avec un bâton s'étant précipité vers lui en criant « Gare! » il avait voulu s'enfuir. C'est tout ce dont il se souvient. On sait le reste. Son sauveur, bien connu de l'entourage sous le nom de Guillaume Apollinaire, pouvait avoir une soixantaine d'années. Il avait gagné la médaille du travail et ses compagnons l'estimaient.

Quand pourrons-nous donner la clé de ce mystère? On recherche, en vain jusqu'à présent, l'entrepreneur et l'architecte de la maison penchée. L'émotion est considérable.

A NOT-VERY-SOLID HOUSE

Watchman Falls Victim to
His Devotion to Duty

For a long time the method used to build an apartment house located on the Rue des Martyrs was deemed unreasonable by the people of the neighborhood. No roofing had appeared but the painters and carpenters had already started to decorate the apartments. Every day new scaffolding propped up the tottering façade, causing great uneasiness among people passing by, whom the watchman reassured. Alas! the latter had to pay for his optimism with his life, because yesterday at twelve-thirty, when the workers were out eating lunch, the masonry caved in, burying him under its rubble.

A child discovered unconscious at the scene of the disaster quickly revived. It was young Hope, seven years old, who was immediately returned to his parents' home. He was more frightened than hurt. The first thing he did was demand the scooter on which he'd sped from the top of the street. The little boy told how a man with a stick had rushed towards him yelling, "Watch out!" which made him want to run away. That's all he remembers. We know the rest. The man who saved him, well known in the surrounding area by the name of Guillaume Apollinaire, was about sixty years old. He had been decorated with a medal for his work, and his friends spoke well of him.

When will we find the key to this mystery? The contractor and the architect of the leaning house are being sought, so far in vain. Feeling is running high.

Le Corset Mystère

Mes belles lectrices,

à force d'en voir **de toutes les Couleurs**
Cartes splendides, *à effets de lumière,* Venise

Autrefois les meubles de ma chambre étaient fixés solidement aux murs et je me faisais attacher pour écrire :
J'ai le pied marin

nous adhérons à une sorte de **Touring Club** sentimental

UN CHATEAU A LA PLACE DE LA TÊTE

c'est aussi le **Bazar de la Charité**
Jeux très amusants pour tous âges ;
Jeux poétiques, etc.

Je tiens Paris comme — pour vous dévoiler l'avenir — votre main ouverte

la taille bien prise.

The Mysterious Corset

My dear lady readers,

because we've seen some in **all colors**
Splendid maps, *highlighted,* Venice

The furniture in my room used to be fastened
solidly to the walls and I'd have myself strapped into it to write
I've found my sea legs

we're members of a kind of emotional **Touring Club**

A CASTLE INSTEAD OF A HEAD

it's also the **Charity Bazaar**
Entertaining games for all ages;
Poetry games, etc.

I hold Paris like—if I may unveil the future to you—
your open hand

her elegant figure.

CLAIR DE TERRE

(1923)

La terre brille dans le ciel comme un astre énorme au milieu des étoiles.

Notre globe projette sur la lune un intense clair de terre.

« Le ciel »
Nouvelle astronomie pour tous.

EARTHLIGHT

(1923)

The earth shines in the sky like a huge star amidst the stars.

Our globe casts an intense earthlight on the moon.

"The Sky"
New Astronomy for Everyone

Au grand poète

SAINT-POL-ROUX

A ceux qui comme lui

s'offrent

LE MAGNIFIQUE

plaisir de se faire oublier

To the great poet
SAINT-POL-ROUX
To those who like him
offer themselves
THE MAGNIFICENT
pleasure of being forgotten

CINQ RÊVES

A Georges de Chirico

I

Je passe le soir dans une rue déserte du quartier des Grands-Augustins quand mon attention est arrêtée par un écriteau au-dessus de la porte d'une maison. Cet écriteau c'est : « ABRI » ou « A LOUER », en tout cas quelque chose qui n'a plus cours. Intrigué j'entre et je m'enfonce dans un couloir extrêmement sombre.

Un personnage, qui fait dans la suite du rêve figure de génie, vient à ma rencontre et me guide à travers un escalier que nous descendons tous deux et qui est très long.

Ce personnage, je l'ai déjà vu. C'est un homme qui s'est occupé autrefois de me trouver une situation.

Aux murs de l'escalier je remarque un certain nombre de reliefs bizarres, que je suis amené à examiner de près, mon guide ne m'adressant pas la parole.

Il s'agit de moulages en plâtre, plus exactement: de moulages de moustaches considérablement grossies.

Voici, entre autres, les moustaches de Baudelaire, de Germain Nouveau et de Barbey d'Aurevilly.

Le génie me quitte sur la dernière marche et je me trouve dans une sorte de vaste hall divisé en trois parties.

Dans la première salle, de beaucoup la plus petite, où pénètre seulement le jour d'un soupirail incompréhensible, un jeune homme est

FIVE DREAMS

To Giorgio de Chirico

I

I'm spending the evening on a deserted street in the Grands-Augustins part of town when my attention is caught by a notice above a house door. This notice is: "SHELTER" or "TO LET," in any case something no longer up to date. Intrigued, I enter and plunge into an extraordinarily dark passageway.

An individual who in the course of the dream gives the impression of being a genius comes to meet me and guides me down a very long stairway that we descend together.

This individual is someone I have seen before. He's a man who once tried to find me a job.

On the stairway walls I notice a number of bizarre reliefs that I am brought over to examine closely while my guide remains silent.

There are plaster casts, more precisely: casts of mustaches, considerably larger than life.

Among others, there are mustaches of Baudelaire, Germain Nouveau, and Barbey d'Aurevilly.

The genius leaves me on the bottom step and I find myself in a kind of vast hall divided into three parts.

In the first room, by far the smallest, where only the daylight from an unfathomable vent penetrates, a young man is seated at a table writing poems. All around him, on the table and on the floor, incredibly soiled manuscripts are profusely scattered. This young man is no

assis à une table et compose des poèmes. Tout autour de lui, sur la table et par terre, sont répandus à profusion des manuscrits extrêmement sales.

Ce jeune homme ne m'est pas inconnu, c'est M. Georges Gabory. La pièce voisine, elle aussi plus que sommairement meublée, est un peu mieux éclairée, quoique d'une façon tout à fait insuffisante.

Dans la même attitude que le premier personnage, mais m'inspirant, par contre, une sympathie réelle, je distingue M. Pierre Reverdy.

Ni l'un ni l'autre n'a paru me voir, et c'est seulement après m'être arrêté tristement derrière eux que je pénètre dans la troisième pièce.

Celle-ci est de beaucoup la plus grande, et les objets s'y trouvent un peu mieux en valeur : un fauteuil inoccupé devant la table paraît m'être destiné; je prends place devant le papier immaculé.

J'obéis à la suggestion et me mets en devoir de composer des poèmes. Mais, tout en m'abandonnant à la spontanéité la plus grande, je n'arrive à écrire sur le premier feuillet que ces mots : La lumière… Celui-ci aussitôt déchiré, sur le second feuillet : La lumière… et sur le troisième feuillet : La lumière…

II

J'étais assis dans le métropolitain en face d'une femme que je n'avais pas autrement remarquée, lorsqu'à l'arrêt du train elle se leva et dit en me regardant : « Vie végétative ». J'hésitai un instant, on était à la station Trocadéro, puis je me levai, décidé à la suivre.

Au haut de l'escalier nous étions dans une immense prairie sur laquelle tombait un jour verdâtre, extrêmement dur, de fin d'après-midi.

stranger to me; it's Mr. Georges Gabory. In the next space, also no more than perfunctorily furnished, the light is a little better, though completely insufficient.

In the same position as the first character, but unlike him inspiring a real sympathy in me, I can see Mr. Pierre Reverdy.

Neither of them appears to have seen me, and it is only after having paused sadly behind them that I push on into the third room.

This is by far the largest, and the objects found there somewhat more valuable: an unoccupied armchair in front of the table seems destined for me; I assume my place in front of the immaculate sheet of paper.

I take the hint and throw myself into the task of writing poems. But, though I abandon myself entirely to the greatest spontaneity, I only manage to write these words on the first page: The light.... The moment this is torn up, on the second page: The light... and on the third page: The light....

II

I was sitting in a metro car opposite a woman I hadn't especially noticed when the train stopped and she got up, and looking straight at me said: "Vegetative life." I hesitated a moment, we were at the Trocadéro station, then I got up, after deciding to follow her.

At the top of the stairs we were in an immense meadow where a late afternoon greenish daylight fell, extremely harsh.

La femme avançait dans la prairie sans se retourner et bientôt un personnage très inquiétant, d'allure athlétique et coiffé d'une casquette, vint à sa rencontre.

Cet homme se détachait d'une équipe de joueurs de football composée de trois personnages. Ils échangèrent quelques mots sans faire attention à moi, puis la femme disparut, et je demeurai dans la prairie à regarder les joueurs qui avaient repris leur partie. J'essayai bien aussi d'attraper le ballon, mais... je n'y parvins qu'une fois.

III

Je me baignais avec un petit enfant au bord de la mer. Peu après je me trouvai sur la plage en compagnie d'un certain nombre de gens, dont les uns me sont connus, les autres inconnus, quand brusquement l'un des promeneurs nous signala deux oiseaux qui volaient parallèlement à une certaine distance, et qui pouvaient être des mouettes.

Quelqu'un eut aussitôt l'idée de tirer sur ces oiseaux (car nous portions tous des fusils) et l'on put croire que l'un d'eux avait été blessé.

Ils tombèrent en effet assez loin du rivage, et nous attendîmes quelque temps que la vague les apportât.

A mesure qu'ils approchaient, j'observai que ces animaux n'étaient nullement des oiseaux comme je l'avais cru tout d'abord, mais bien plutôt des sortes de vaches ou de chevaux.

L'animal qui n'était pas blessé soutenait l'autre avec beaucoup d'attendrissement. Quand ils furent à nos pieds, ce dernier expira.

La particularité la plus remarquable que présentait cet animal qui venait de mourir était la différenciation très curieuse de ses yeux.

The woman walked into the meadow without turning around and soon a very disturbing individual with an athletic gait and a cap on his head came to meet her. This man stepped from a team of soccer players composed of three individuals. They exchanged a few words without paying attention to me, then the woman disappeared, and I stayed in the meadow to watch the players, who had started their game again. I also tried very hard to catch the ball, but... I could only manage it once.

III

I was swimming with a small child at the seashore. A little later I found myself on the beach in the company of a number of people, some of whom I know, others I don't, when suddenly one of the strollers directed our attention to two birds, which could have been gulls, flying parallel at some distance.

Immediately someone had the idea of shooting these birds (since we were all carrying rifles) and it looked as though one of the two had been wounded.

They fell quite far from shore in fact, and we waited a while for the waves to carry them in.

As they approached, I noticed that these animals weren't birds at all, as I had first thought, but rather were some kind of cow or horse.

The animal that wasn't wounded held up the other very tenderly. When they were at our feet, the latter expired.

The most remarkable detail exhibited by this animal that had just died was the most curious differentiation of its eyes.

L'un de ceux-ci, en effet, était complètement terne et assez semblable à une coquille d'oursin, tandis que l'autre était merveilleusement coloré et brillant.

L'animal secourable avait depuis longtemps disparu. C'est alors que M. Roger Lefébure qui, je ne sais pourquoi, se trouvait parmi nous, s'empara de l'œil phosphorescent et le prit pour monocle.

Ce que voyant une personne de l'assistance jugea bon de rapporter l'anecdote suivante :

Dernièrement, comme à son habitude, M. Paul Poiret dansait devant ses clientes, quand brusquement son monocle tomba par terre et se brisa. M. Paul Eluard, qui se trouvait là, eut l'amabilité de lui offrir le sien, mais celui-ci subit le même sort.

IV

Une partie de ma matinée s'était passée à conjuguer un nouveau temps du verbe être — car on venait d'inventer un nouveau temps du verbe être. Au cours de l'après-midi j'avais écrit un article qu'autant que je me rappelle je trouvais peu profond mais assez brillant. Un peu plus tard je m'étais mis à continuer d'écrire un roman. Cette dernière entreprise m'avait conduit à effectuer des recherches dans ma bibliothèque. Elles amenèrent bientôt la découverte d'un ouvrage in-8° que j'ignorais posséder et qui se composait de plusieurs tomes. J'ouvris l'un d'eux au hasard. Le livre se présentait comme un traité de philosophie mais, à la place du titre correspondant à une des divisions générales de l'ouvrage, comme j'aurais lu : Logique, ou : Morale, je lus ; *Enigmatique*. Le texte m'échappe entièrement, je n'ai souvenir que des planches figurant invariablement un personnage ecclésiastique ou

One of them, in fact, was completely leaden and quite like a sea-urchin's shell, while the other was marvelously colored and shining.

The helpful animal had long since disappeared. It was then that Mr. Roger Lefebure, who—I don't know why—found himself among us, seized the phosphorescent eye and used it as a monocle.

Seeing this, one of the onlookers thought it fitting to report the following anecdote:

Recently, as is his custom, Mr. Paul Poiret was dancing in front of one of his female clients, when suddenly his monocle fell to the ground and broke. Mr. Paul Éluard, who was also there, had the courtesy to offer him his own, but it suffered the same fate.

IV

A part of my morning had been spent conjugating a new tense of the verb to be—because a new tense of the verb to be had just been invented. In the course of the afternoon I had written an article that, as far as I can remember, I found shallow but fairly brilliant. A little later I went back to work on a novel I was writing. This last enterprise had led me to do some research in my library. This soon led to the discovery of a work in octavo, composed of several volumes, that I didn't know I owned. I opened one of them at random. The book claimed to be a philosophical treatise, but in one section, instead of Logic or Ethics, the heading read: *Enigmatic.* The text completely escapes me, I have only the memory of illustrations invariably representing an ecclesiastical or mythological character in the middle of an immense waxed room that looked like the Apollo Gallery. The walls and the parquet floor reflected better than mirrors since each of these

mythologique au milieu d'une salle cirée immense qui ressemblait à la galerie d'Apollon. Les murs et le parquet réfléchissaient mieux que des glaces puisque chacun de ces personnages se retrouvait plusieurs fois dans la pièce sous diverses attitudes avec la même intensité et le même relief et qu'Adonis, par exemple, était couché à ses propres pieds. Je me sentais en proie à une grande exaltation ; il me semblait qu'un livre d'observations médicales en ma possession m'apporterait sur la question qui me préoccupait une véritable révélation. J'y trouvai en effet ce que je cherchais : une photographie de femme brune un peu forte, ni très belle ni très jeune, que je connaissais vaguement. J'étais assis chez moi, à la table de l'atelier, le dos tourné à la fenêtre. La femme de la photographie vint alors frôler mon épaule droite et, après m'avoir adressé quelques paroles comminatoires, elle alla poser la main gauche sur la corniche de la petite armoire située près de la porte et je ne la vis plus. Je poursuivis mes investigations : il s'agissait maintenant de chercher dans le dictionnaire un mot qui était probablement le mot : souris. J'ouvris à Rh et mon attention fut aussitôt attirée par la figure qui accompagnait le mot : rhéostat. On y voyait un petit nombre de parachutes ou de nuages suspendus ensemble à la manière des ballons d'enfants : dans chaque parachute ou dans chaque nuage il y avait, accroupi, un Chinois. Je crus avoir trouvé ensuite ce qui m'était nécessaire à : rongeur. Mais déjà, je n'avais plus grande attention à donner de ce côté. Devant le piano, en face de moi, se tenait en effet M. Charles Baron, jeune homme que dans la réalité je n'arrive jamais à reconnaître, vêtu de noir et avec une certaine recherche. Avant que j'eusse pu lui demander compte de sa présence, Louis Aragon l'avait déjà remplacé. Il venait me persuader de l'obligation de sortir immédiatement avec lui : je le suivais. Au bas de l'escalier, nous étions avenue des

characters could be found any number of times in the room in various positions, with the same vividness and the same relief, and Adonis, for example, was lying at his own feet. I felt myself in the grip of a great exaltation; it seemed to me that a book of medical observations in my possession would bring me to a true revelation concerning the question that had preoccupied me. In fact I found what I was looking for in it: a photograph of a somewhat heavy brunette, neither very pretty nor very young, whom I vaguely knew. I was sitting at home, at my workroom table, back to the window. The woman in the photograph then came in and lightly touched my right shoulder and, after addressing some threatening words to me, placed her left hand on the edge of the small dresser located near the door and I could no longer see her. I pursued my investigations: now it was important to look up a word in the dictionary that was probably the word: mouse. I opened to Rh and my attention was immediately caught by the figure which accompanied the word: rheostat. Pictured there were a few parachutes or clouds clustered together like children's balloons: in each parachute or in each cloud was a Chinese man, squatting. I then believed I had found what I'd been looking for: rodent. But my attention was already straying elsewhere. In fact, facing me in front of the piano stood Mr. Charles Baron, a young man whom in reality I never seem to recognize, dressed in black and with a certain studied elegance. Before I could ask him why he was there, Louis Aragon had already taken his place. He came to convince me that I should accompany him immediately: I followed him. At the bottom of the stairway we were on the Avenue des Champs-Elysées, walking up towards the Étoile where, according to Aragon, we had to arrive at all costs before eight o'clock. Each of us carried an empty picture frame. Beneath the Arc de Tri-

Champs-Élysées, montant vers l'Étoile où, d'après Aragon, nous devions à tout prix arriver avant huit heures. Nous portions chacun un cadre vide. Sous l'Arc de Triomphe je ne songeais qu'à me débarrasser du mien, la pendule marquait sept heures vingt-neuf. Aragon, lui, objectait le risque de pluie, il voulait absolument que les cadres fussent à l'abri. Nous finîmes par les placer sous la protection des moulures supérieures, contre la pierre, légèrement inclinés, à hauteur de chevalet. Il était question, je crois, de venir les reprendre plus tard. Au moment où nous les disposions j'observai que le cadre d'Aragon était doré, le mien blanc avec de très anciennes traces de dorures, de dimensions sensiblement moins grandes.

V

Paul Eluard, Marcel Noll et moi nous trouvons réunis à la campagne dans une pièce où trois objets sollicitent notre attention : un livre fermé et un livre ouvert, d'assez grandes dimensions, de l'épaisseur d'un atlas et inclinés sur une sorte de pupitre à musique, qui tient aussi d'un autel. Noll tourne les pages du livre ouvert sans parvenir à nous intéresser. En ce qui me concerne, je ne m'occupe que du troisième objet, un appareil métallique de construction très simple, que je vois pour la première fois et dont j'ignore l'usage, mais qui est extrêmement brillant. Je suis tenté de l'emporter mais, l'ayant pris en mains, je m'aperçois qu'il est étiqueté 9 fr. 90. Il disparaît d'ailleurs à ce moment et est remplacé par Philippe Soupault, en grand pardessus de voyage blanc, chapeau blanc, souliers blancs, etc. Soupault est pressé de nous quitter, il s'excuse aimablement et j'essaie en vain de le retenir. Nous le regardons par la fenêtre s'éloigner en compagnie de sa femme, que nous ne

omphe my only thought was to get rid of mine; the clock said seven twenty-nine. Aragon himself objected that there was a good chance of rain, he absolutely wanted the picture frames to be protected. We ended up putting them under the shelter of the upper moldings, against the stone, at a slight angle, easel-high. I think we discussed coming to get them later. At the moment when we arranged them I noticed that Aragon's frame was gilded, mine white with very old traces of gilding, and of appreciably smaller dimensions.

V

Paul Éluard, Marcel Noll and I find ourselves together in the country in a room where three objects attract our attention: a closed book and an open book of rather large dimensions, as thick as atlases and lying on a kind of music stand that serves as an altar. Noll turns the pages of the open book without managing to interest us. As for me, I'm only interested in the third object, a metallic machine of the simplest construction, highly polished, that I've never seen before and whose purpose I don't understand. I'm tempted to carry it away but, having taken it in my hands, I notice that it's labeled 9 Fr. 90. At that moment, however, it disappears and is replaced by Philippe Soupault, in a big white travel coat, white hat, white shoes, etc. Soupault is in a hurry to leave us, he excuses himself cordially and I try to detain him. We watch him through the window walking off together with his wife, whom we only see from behind and who, like him, is dressed completely in white. Without looking to find out what has become of Noll, Éluard and I leave the house. Éluard asking me to go hunting with him. He carries a bow and arrows. We come to the edge of a pond

voyons que de dos et qui est comme lui toute habillée de blanc. Sans chercher à savoir ce que Noll est devenu, Eluard et moi, nous quittons alors la maison. Eluard me demandant de l'accompagner à la chasse. Il emporte un arc et des flèches. Nous arrivons au bord d'un étang couvert de faisanes. « A la bonne heure », dis-je à Eluard. Mais lui : « Cher ami, ne crois pas que je sois venu ici pour ces faisanes, je cherche tout autre chose, je cherche François. Tu vas voir François. » Alors toutes les faisanes d'appeler : « François, François, François! » Et je distingue au milieu de l'étang un superbe faisan doré. Eluard décoche dans sa direction plusieurs flèches mais — ici l'idée de la maladresse prend en quelque sorte possession du rêve qu'elle n'abandonnera plus — les flèches portent « trop court ». Pourtant le faisan doré finit par être atteint. A la place de ses ailes se fixent alors deux petites boîtes rectangulaires de papier rose qui flottent un instant sur l'eau après que l'oiseau a disparu. Nous ne bougeons plus jusqu'à ce qu'une femme nue, très belle, s'élève lentement de l'eau, le plus loin possible de nous. Nous la voyons à mi-corps puis à mi-jambes. Elle chante. A ma grande émotion, Eluard lance vers elle plusieurs traits qui ne l'atteignent pas mais voici que la femme, qu'une seconde nous avions perdue de vue, émerge de l'eau tout près de nous. Une nouvelle flèche vient lui transpercer le sein. Elle y porte la main d'un geste adorable et se reprend à chanter. Sa voix s'affaiblit lentement. Je n'ai pas plus tôt cessé de l'entendre qu'Eluard et elle ne sont plus là. Je me trouve en présence de petits hommes mesurant environ 1m. 10 et habillés de jersey bleu. Ils arrivent de tous les points de l'étang et, comme je les observe sans défiance, l'un d'eux, ayant l'air d'accomplir un rite, s'apprête à m'enfoncer dans le mollet une très petite flèche à deux pointes. Il me semble qu'on veut m'unir dans la mort au faisan doré et à la belle

covered with hen-pheasants. "Right on time," I say to Éluard. But he: "My friend, don't think I've come here for these hen-pheasants! I'm looking for something else altogether, I'm looking for François. You're going to see François." Then all the hen-pheasants called out: "François, François, François!" And in the middle of the pond I noticed a superb cock-pheasant. Éluard lets fly many arrows in its direction but—here the feeling of awkwardness somehow takes possession of the dream and will not go away—the arrows "fall short." Nevertheless the golden pheasant ends up being hit. Instead of wings it has fastened to it two little rectangular boxes of pink paper that float for a moment on the water after the bird has disappeared. We don't make a move until a naked woman, quite lovely, rises slowly from the water, as far away as possible from us. We see her down to the waist, then to the knees. She is singing. To my great excitement, Éluard launches several shafts at her that don't reach her but now the woman, whom we've lost sight of for a second, emerges from the water right beside us. A new arrow has just pierced her breast. She touches it with her hand in a charming gesture and begins to sing again. Her voice slowly grows weaker. No sooner do I stop hearing it than Éluard and she are no longer there. I find myself in the presence of little men measuring about 3½ feet tall and dressed in blue jersey. They come from all over the pond and, as I watch without suspicion, one of them, with the air of performing a ritual, prepares to stick a tiny two-pointed arrow into my calf. It seems to me that they want to unite me in death with the golden pheasant and the beautiful singer. I struggle and knock several of the little blue men to the ground. But the little sacrificer chases me and I end up falling into a thicket where, with the help of one of the other pursuers, he tries to tie me up. It

chanteuse. Je me débats et j'envoie à terre plusieurs des petits hommes bleus. Mais le petit sacrificateur me poursuit et je finis par tomber dans un buisson où, avec l'aide d'un des autres poursuivants, il cherche à me ligoter. Il me semble facile de terrasser mes deux adversaires et de les ligoter à ma place mais la maladresse ne me permet que de leur prendre la corde et d'en faire autour de leur corps un nœud extrêmement lâche. Je m'enfuis ensuite le long d'une voie de chemin de fer, et, comme on ne me poursuit plus, je modère peu à peu mon allure. Je passe à proximité d'une charmante usine que traverse un fil télégraphique dirigé perpendiculairement à la voie et situé à cinq ou six mètres du sol. Un homme de ma taille tend à deux reprises, très énergiquement, le bras vers le fil sur lequel, sans aucun mouvement de lancement, il réussit à placer en équilibre, à égale distance de l'usine et des rails, deux verres vides du type gobelet. « C'est, dit-il, pour les oiseaux. » Je repars, avec l'idée de gagner la gare encore lointaine d'où je puisse prendre le train pour Paris. J'arrive enfin sur le quai d'une ville qui est un peu Nantes et n'est pas tout à fait Versailles, mais où je ne suis plus du tout dépaysé. Je sais qu'il me faut tourner à droite et longer le fleuve assez longtemps. J'observe, au-dessus du très beau pont qui se trouve à ma gauche, les évolutions inquiétantes d'un avion, d'abord très élevé, qui boucle la boucle avec peine et inélégance. Il perd constamment de sa hauteur et n'est plus guère qu'au niveau des tourelles des maisons. C'est d'ailleurs moins un avion qu'un gros wagon noir. Il faut que le pilote soit fou pour renouveler sa prouesse si bas. Je m'attends à le voir s'écraser sur le pont. Mais l'appareil s'abîme dans le fleuve et il en sort sain et sauf un des petits hommes bleus de tout à l'heure qui gagne la berge à la nage, passe près de moi sans paraître me remarquer et s'éloigne dans le sens opposé au mien.

seems easy for me to floor my two adversaries and tie them up in my place but all my clumsiness allows me to do is grab the rope and knot it incredibly loosely around their bodies. I then escape along a railroad track, and, since they have stopped following me, I slacken my pace bit by bit. I pass close to a charming factory spanned by a telegraph wire strung at a right angle to the track and located fifteen or twenty feet from the ground. A man of my size stretches his arm twice very energetically towards the wire on which, without any throwing motion, he succeeds in balancing, at an equal distance from the factory and the rails, two empty goblet-type glasses. "It's for the birds," he says. I set out again, with the idea of reaching the still distant station where I should be able to catch the train for Paris. I finally arrive at the platform of a city which is a little bit Nantes and not entirely Versailles, but where I am no longer completely out of my element. I know I have to turn right and keep to the river for quite some time. I watch, above the very beautiful bridge on my left, the disturbing maneuvers of an airplane, first quite high up, that loops the loop with difficulty and with elegance. It is steadily losing altitude and is barely above the level of the house-turrets. Moreover, it's less an airplane than a big black railroad car. The pilot must be crazy to repeat his stunts so low. I expect to see him crash onto the bridge. But the machine is swallowed up in the river and out of it, safe and sound, comes one of the little blue men from a short while ago who reaches the river bank swimming, goes by near me without appearing to notice me, and walks away in the direction opposite mine.

PIÈCE FAUSSE

A Benjamin Péret

Du vase en cristal de Bohême
Du vase en cris
Du vase en cris
Du vase en
En cristal
Du vase en cristal de Bohême
Bohême
Bohême
En cristal de Bohême
Bohême
Bohême
Bohême
Hême hême oui Bohême
Du vase en cristal de Bo Bo
Du vase en cristal de Bohême
Aux bulles qu'enfant tu soufflais
Tu soufflais
Tu soufflais
Flais
Flais
Tu soufflais
Qu'enfant tu soufflais
Du vase en cristal de Bohême
Aux bulles qu'enfant tu soufflais

COUNTERFEIT COIN

To Benjamin Péret

From the vase of crystal made in Bohemia
From the vase of cry
From the vase of cry
From the vase of
Of crystal
From the vase of crystal made in Bohemia
Bohemia
Bohemia
Of crystal made in Bohemia
Bohemia
Bohemia
Bohemia
Hem hem yes Bohemia
From the vase of crystal made in Bo Bo
From the vase of crystal made in Bohemia
To the bubbles you blew as a child
You blew
You blew
Ew
Ew
You blew
You blew as a child
From the vase of crystal made in Bohemia
To the bubbles you blew as a child

Tu soufflais
Tu soufflais
Oui qu'enfant tu soufflais
C'est là c'est là tout le poème
Aube éphé
Aube éphé
Aube éphémère de reflets
Aube éphé
Aube éphé
Aube éphémère de reflets

You blew
You blew
Yes you blew as a child
That's it that's it the whole poem
Emeral dawn
Emeral dawn
Reflections' ephemeral dawn
Emeral dawn
Emeral dawn
Reflections' ephemeral dawn

PSTT

Neuilly 1–18 ....Breton, vacherie modèle, r. de l'Ouest, 12, Neuilly.

Nord 13–40 ....Breton (E.), mon. funèbr., av. Cimetière Parisien, 23, Pantin.

Passy 44–15 ....Breton (Eug.), vins, restaur., tabacs, r. de la Pompe, 176.

Roquette 07–90 ...Breton (François), vétérinaire, r. Trousseau, 21, (11e)

Central 64–99 ......Breton frères, mécaniciens, r. de Belleville, 262, (20e).

Bergère 43–61 .....Breton et fils, r. Rougemont, 12, (9e).

Archives 32–58 ....Breton (G.), fournit. cycles, autos, r. des Archives, 78, (3e).

Central 30–08 ......Breton (Georges), r. du Marché-Saint-Honoré, 4, (1er).

Wagram 60–84 ....Breton M. et Mme G.), bd Malesherbes, 58, (8e).

Gutenberg 03–78.Breton (H.), dentelles, r. de Richelieu, 60, (2e).

Passy 80–70 ....Breton (Henri), négociant, r. Octave-Feuillet, (16e).

Gobelins 08–09 ...Breton (J.), Elix. Combier, ag. gén., butte du Rhône, 21–23.

Roquette 32–59 ...Breton (J.-L.), député, s.-secr. Etat, inv., bd Soult, 81 bis.

Archives 39–43 ....Breton (L.), hôtel-bar, r. François-Miron, 38, (4e).

Marcadet 04–11 ..Breton (Noël), hôtel-rest., bd National, 56 Clichy.

PSST

Neuilly 1–18 ....Breton, model dairy, 12 R. de l'Ouest, Neuilly.

Nord 13–40..........Breton (E.) fun. monum., 23 Ave. Cimitière Parisien, Pantin.

Passy 44–15..........Breton (Eug.), wines, rest., cigars, 176 R. de la Pompe.

Roquette 07–90 ....Breton (François), veterinarian, 21 R. Trousseau, (11th).

Central 64–99 ....Breton Bros., engineers, 262 R. de Belleville (20th).

Bergère 43–61 ....Breton and Son, 12 R. Rougement, (9th).

Archives 32–58 ......Breton (G.), automotive, cycle suppl., 78 R. des Archives, (3rd).

Central 30–08 ....Breton (Georges), 4 R. due Marché-Saint-Honoré, (1st).

Wagram 60–84 ......Breton (Mr. and Mrs. G.), 58 Blvd. Malesherbes, (8th).

Gutenberg 03–78 ..Breton (H.), laces, 60 R. de Richelieu, (2nd).

Passy 80–70............Breton (Henri), wholesaler, 22 R. Octave-Feuillet, (16th).

Gobelins 08–09......Breton (J.), Combier Elix., main off., 21-23 Butte du Rhône.

Roquette 32–59......Breton (J.-L.), rcpresentative, undr.-secr. State, inviol., 8½ Blvd. Soult.

Archives 39–43 ......Breton (L.), hotel-bar, 38 R. François-Miron, (4th).

Marcadet 04–11 ....Breton (Noel), hotel-rest., 56 Blvd. National, Clichy.

Roquette 02–25...Breton (Paul), décolleteur, r. Saint-Maur, 21 (11ᵉ).
Central 84–08......Breton (Th.), contentieux, r.du fg. Montmartre 13, (9ᵉ).
Saxe 57–86..........Breton (J.), biscuits, r. La Quintinie, 16–18, (15ᵉ).
Archives 35–44....Breton (J.) et Cie, papiers en gros, r. Saint-Martin, 245, (3ᵉ).
Roquette 09–76...Breton et Cie (Soc. an.) charbons gros, q. La Râpée, 60, (12ᵉ).

Breton (André).

Roquette 02–25......Breton (Paul), lathe operator, 21 R. Saint-Maur, (11th).

Central 84–08 ....Breton (Th.), law office, 13 R. du Fg. Montmartre, (9th).

Saxe 57–86..............Breton (J.), cookies, 16-18 R. La Quintinie, (15th).

Archives 35–44 ......Breton (J.) and Co., wholesale paper, 245 R. Saint-Martin, (3rd).

Roquette 09–76......Breton and Co., Inc., wholesale coal, Q. La Rapée, 60 (12th).

Breton (André)

LES REPTILES CAMBRIOLEURS

A Janine

Sur la tringle de la cour la petite Marie venait de mettre le linge à sécher. C'était une succession de dates fraîches encore : celle du mariage de sa mère (la belle robe de noce avait été mise en pièces), un baptême, les rideaux du berceau du petit frère riaient au vent comme des mouettes sur les rochers de la côte. L'enfant soufflait les fleurs de la lessive comme des chandelles et se persuadait de la lenteur de la vie. Elle se prenait de temps à autre à regarder ses mains un peu trop roses et se renversait dans l'eau du baquet pour plus tard, quand elle aurait une anémone à la ceinture. Il commençait à faire nuit. Les précisions des cartes de marine ne comptaient plus guère; sur les ponts traînaient des écharpes de fumée ocre et des adieux. Sur le « sarrau » couvert d'étincelles de lait passent successivement la paresse des distractions, la tempête de l'amour et les nombreuses nuées d'insectes du souci. Marie sait que sa mère ne jouit plus de toutes ses facultés : des journées entières, coiffée de réflexions plus coulissées qu'en rêve, elle mord le collier de larmes du rire. Se souvient-elle d'avoir été belle? Les plus anciens habitants de la contrée s'inquiétaient du retour des couvreurs sur la ville, on eût préféré la pluie dans les maisons. Mais ce ciel ! Les ruches d'illusions s'emplissent d'un poison étrange à mesure que la jeune femme élève les bras vers la tête pour dire : laissez- moi. Elle demande à boire du lait de volcan et on lui apporte de l'eau minérale. Elle joint les mains avant de prendre une feuille, plus verte que la lumière des carafes, pour écrire. Par-dessous l'épaule on écoute (les anges ne s'en font pas faute, quand ils arrivent guidés par

THE REPTILE HOUSEBURGLARS

To Janine

On the clothes reel in the courtyard little Marie had just hung out the laundry to dry. It was a succession of still-recent dates: that of her mother's marriage (the beautiful wedding dress now torn to pieces), a baptism, the curtains of her little brother's crib laughed in the wind like seagulls on the crags of the coast. The little girl blew out the detergent flowers like candles and convinced herself how slow life was. She started now and then to look at her slightly too-pink hands, and leaned back into the bucket of water for later on, when she'd have an anemone in her belt. Night began to fall. The details of nautical charts hardly mattered anymore; on the bridges, scarves of ochre smoke and goodbyes trailed on the ground. The laziness of distractions, the tempest of love, and numerous marigold insect storm clouds pass in succession across the "overalls" covered with sparks of milk. Marie knows that her mother is no longer in possession of all her faculties: for days at a time, her head covered with reflections more notched than in dreams, she bites laughter's necklace of tears. Does she remember having been beautiful? The people who'd lived in the region the longest were worried that the roofers would return to the town, they'd have preferred rain in their houses. But the sky! As the hives of illusion fill with strange poison, the young woman brings her arms up towards her head to say: leave me alone. She asks for a drink of volcano milk and they bring her mineral water. She folds her hands before picking a leaf, greener than the light of carafes, to write on. Underneath her shoulder we hear (the angels don't miss it when they

la trace des plumes qu'elle ne porte plus) : « Ma petite Marie, tu sauras un jour quel sacrifice est à la veille de se consommer, je ne t'en dis pas davantage. Va, ma fille, sois heureuse. Les yeux de mon enfant sont des rideaux plus tendres que ceux des chambres d'hôtel où j'ai demeuré en compagnie des aviateurs et des plantes vertes. » Le trésor enfoui dans la cendre de la cheminée se décompose en petits insectes phosphorescents qui font entendre un chant monotone, mais que pourrait-elle dire aux grillons? Dieu ne se sentait pas plus aimé qu'à l'ordinaire mais le candélabre des arbres fleuris était là pour quelque chose, il s'y blottissait de frivoles démons changeants comme l'eau des sources qui court sur le satin des pierres et le velours noir des poissons. A quoi Marie se montre-t-elle soudain si attentive? On est au mois d'août et les automobiles ont émigré depuis le Grand Prix. Qui va-t-on voir apparaître dans ce quartier solitaire, le poète qui fuit sa demeure en modulant sa plainte par les rails de perle, l'amoureux qui court rejoindre sa belle sur un éclair ou le chasseur tapi dans les herbes coupantes et qui a froid? L'enfant donne sa langue au chat, elle brûle de connaître ce qu'elle ignore, la signification de ce long vol à ras de terre, le beau ruisseau coupable qui commence à courir. Mon Dieu, mais voici qu'elle tombe à genoux et les gémissements se font moins sourds à l'étage supérieur, l'œil de bœuf reflète tout ce qui se passe et une âme monte au ciel. On ne sait rien; le trèfle à quatre feuilles s'entrouvre aux rayons de la lune, il n'y a plus qu'à entrer pour les constatations dans la maison vide.

arrive, guided by the trail of feathers she no longer wears): "Marie dear, one day you'll know what a sacrifice is on the verge of being consummated, I won't tell you anymore about it. Go, my daughter, be happy. My child's eyes are curtains more tender than those in the hotel rooms where I lived in the company of aviators and green plants." The treasure buried in the fireplace ash decomposes into little phosphorescent insects that utter a monotonous song, but what could she say to the crickets? God didn't feel more loved than usual but the candelabra of trees in bloom were there for a reason. Frivolous demons hid, changeable as spring waters that rush over the satin of stones and the black velvet of fish. What did Marie suddenly appear so attentive to? It's the month of August, and the cars have emigrated since the Grand Prix. Whom are we going to see appear in this lonely part of town, the poet running away from home modulating his lament over the pearl rails, the man in love running to catch up with his beauty on a thunderbolt, or the hunter crouched in grass that can cut you, and who is cold? The little girl throws in the towel, she's burning to know what she doesn't, the meaning of this long flight at ground level, the beautiful guilty stream that begins to flow. My God, and now she falls to her knees and on the floor above, the moans become less muffled, the face of the wall clock reflects everything that happens and a soul rises to heaven. Who knows; the four-leaf clover half opens to the moon's rays; for the evidence you need only enter the empty house.

AMOUR PARCHEMINÉ

Quand les fenêtres comme l'œil du chacal et le désir percent l'aurore, des treuils de soie me hissent sur les passerelles de la banlieue. J'appelle une fille qui rêve dans la maisonnette dorée ; elle me rejoint sur les tas de mousse noire et m'offre ses lèvres qui sont des pierres au fond de la rivière rapide. Des pressentiments voilés descendent les marches des édifices. Le mieux est de fuir les grands cylindres de plume quand les chasseurs boitent dans les terres détrempées. Si l'on prend un bain dans la moire des rues, l'enfance revient au pays, levrette grise. L'homme cherche sa proie dans les airs et les fruits sèchent sur des claies de papier rose, à l'ombre des noms démesurés par l'oubli. Les joies et les peines se répandent dans la ville. L'or et l'eucalyptus, de même odeur, attaquent les rêves. Parmi les freins et les edelweiss sombres se reposent des formes souterraines semblables à des bouchons de parfumeurs.

SHRIVELLED LOVE

When windows pierce dawn like desire and the jackal's eye, silk winches hoist me onto catwalks in the suburbs. I call to a girl dreaming in the gilded cottage; she overtakes me on heaps of black moss and offers me her lips which are stones at the bottom of the swift stream. Veiled threats walk down building steps. The best thing to do is to run away from the great feather cylinders when hunters limp across sodden fields. If we bathe in the watered silk of the streets, childhood returns to its homeland, a female greyhound. Man hunts his prey in the air and fruits dry on trays of pink paper, in the shadow of names magnified by forgetfulness. Joys and sorrows spread through the city. Gold and eucalyptus, with the same odor, attack our dreams. Among bridles and gloomy edelweiss lie underground shapes like stoppers on bottles of perfume.

CARTES SUR LES DUNES

A Giuseppe Ungaretti

L'horaire des fleurs creuses et des pommettes saillantes nous invite à quitter les salières volcaniques pour les baignoires d'oiseaux. Sur une serviette damée rouge sont disposés les jours de l'année. L'air n'est plus si pur, la route n'est plus si large que le célèbre clairon. Dans une valise peinte de gros vers on emporte les soirs périssables qui sont la place des genoux sur un prie-Dieu. De petites bicyclettes côtelées tournent sur le comptoir. L'oreille des poissons, plus fourchue que le chèvrefeuille, écoute descendre les huiles bleues. Parmi les burnous éclatants dont la charge se perd dans les rideaux, je reconnais un homme issu de mon sang.

MAPS ON THE DUNES

To Giuseppe Ungaretti

The timetable of hollow flowers and prominent cheekbones invites us to leave volcanic salt-shakers for birdbaths. On a checkerboard napkin the days of the year are arranged. The air is no longer as pure, the road no longer as wide as the famous bugle. Perishable evenings, the place on a prie-dieu where knees go, are carried in a suitcase painted with fat wormy verses. Little corduroy bicycles revolve on the countertop. The fishes' ear, more forked than honeysuckle, hears blue oils coming down. Among sparkling burnouses whose charge gets lost in the curtains, I recognize a man who's blood of my blood.

ÉPERVIER INCASSABLE

A Gala Eluard

La ronde accomplit dans les dortoirs ses ordinaires tours de passe-passe. La nuit, deux fenêtres multicolores restent entrouvertes. Par la première s'introduisent les vices aux noirs sourcils, à l'autre les jeunes pénitentes vont se pencher. Rien ne troublerait autrement la jolie menuiserie du sommeil. On voit des mains se couvrir de manchons d'eau. Sur les grands lits vides s'enchevêtrent des ronces tandis que les oreillers flottent sur des silences plus apparents que réels. A minuit, la chambre souterraine s'étoile vers les théâtres de genre où les jumelles tiennent le principal rôle. Le jardin est rempli de timbres nickelés. Il y a un message au lieu d'un lézard sous chaque pierre.

UNBREAKABLE FISHNET

To Gala Éluard

The nightwatch performs its usual now-you-see-it-now-you-don'ts in the dormitories. At night two multicolored windows are left half open. Through the first, vices with black eyebrows creep in, young women doing penance go to the other to lean out. Otherwise nothing could disturb the pretty woodwork of sleep. We see hands putting on muffs of water. Blackberry bushes get tangled up on big empty beds while white pillows float on silences more apparent than real. At midnight the underground room fills with stars around the theaters, the ones where opera glasses play the leading roles. The garden's filled with nickel-plated bells. There's a message instead of a lizard beneath every stone.

MÉMOIRES D'UN EXTRAIT DES ACTIONS DE CHEMINS.

MEMOIRS OF
A HIGHWAY
STOCK
CERTIFICATE.

A Francis Picabia

C'est aussi le bagne avec ses brèches blondes comme un livre sur les genoux d'une jeune fille
Tantôt il est fermé et crève de peine future sur les remous d'une mer à pic
Un long silence a suivi ces meurtres
L'argent se dessèche sur les rochers
Puis sous une apparence de beauté ou de raison contre toute apparence aussi
Et les deux mains dans une seule palme
On voit le soir
Tomber collier de perles des monts
Sur l'esprit de ces peuplades tachetées règne un amour si plaintif
Que les devins se prennent à ricaner bien haut sur les ponts de fer
Les petites statues se donnent la main à travers la ville
C'est la Nouvelle Quelque Chose travaillé au socle et à l'archet de l'arche
L'air est taillé comme un diamant
Pour les peignes de l'immense Vierge en proie à des vertiges d'essence alcoolique ou florale
La douce cataracte gronde de parfums sur les travaux

To Francis Picabia

That's prison too with its cracks blond as a book on a little girl's lap
Soon it's shut and dying of some future punishment on the eddies of a craggy sea
A long silence followed these murders
Money dries up on the rocks
Then under a semblance of beauty or reason despite any semblance of them
And with our two hands making one palm
We see evening
Falling a necklace of mountain pearls
Over the spirit of these small mottled tribes rules a love so plaintive
That fortune-tellers begin to snicker high up on iron bridges
Little statues join hands across the city
That's the New Whatever worked into the pedestal and arc of the arch
The air is cut like a diamond
For the combs of the immense Virgin prey to vertigos of alcoholic or floral essence
The gentle cataract rumbles with perfumes on the road repairs

RENDEZ-VOUS

A T. Fraenkel

Après les tempêtes cerclées de verre, l'éclair à l'armure brouillée et cette enjambée silencieuse sous laquelle la montagne ouvre des yeux plus fascinants que le Siam, petite fille, adoratrice du pays calqué sur tes parfums, tu vas surprendre l'éveil des chercheurs dans un air révolutionné par le platine. De loin la statue rose qui porte à bout de bras une sorte de bouteille fumant dans un panier regarde par-dessus son épaule errer les anciens vanniers et acrobates. Un joli bagne d'artistes où des zèbres bleus, fouettés par les soupirs qui s'enroulent le soir autour des arbres, exécutent sans fin leur numéro! D'étonnants faisceaux, formés au bord des routes avec les bobines d'azur et le télégraphe, répondent de ta sécurité. Là, dans la lumière profane, les seins éclatant sous un globe de rosée et t'abandonnant à la glissière infinie, à travers les bambous froids tu verras passer le Prince Vandale. L'occasion brûlera aux quatre vents de soufre, de cadmium, de sel et de Bengale. Le bombyx à tête humaine étouffera peu à peu les arlequins maudits et les grandes catastrophes ressusciteront pêle-mêle, pour se résorber dans la bague au chaton vide que je t'ai donnée et qui te tuera.

RENDEZVOUS

To T. Fraenkel

After hurricanes ringed with glass, lightning with jumbled armor and that silent stride under which the mountain opens eyes more fascinating than Siam, little girl, worshipper of the country copied from your perfumes, you're going to surprise the seekers' waking in an air revolutionized by platinum. From a distance the pink statue carrying at arm's length a kind of smoking bottle in a basket looks over its shoulder at ex-basket weavers and acrobats wandering. A fine prison for artists where blue zebras, whipped by sighs that wind the evening around the trees, endlessly perform their number! Some astonishing bundles, fashioned at the sides of the roads with bobbins of azure and the telegraph, answer for your safety. There, in the profane light, your breasts sparkling under a globe of dew and giving yourself up to the endless slide, through the cold bamboos you'll see the Vandal Prince go by. The event will burn in the four winds of sulphur, cadmium, salt, and Bengal light. Little by little the human-headed bombyx will suffocate cursed harlequins and the great catastrophes will come back to life pell-mell, to reabsorb themselves in the ring with the empty setting that I gave you and which will kill you.

PRIVÉ

Coiffé d'une cape beige, il caracole sur l'affiche de satin où deux plumes de paradis lui tiennent lieu d'éperons. Elle, de ses jointures spéciales en haut des airs part la chanson des espèces rayonnantes. Ce qui reste du moteur sanglant est envahi par l'aubépine : à cette heure les premiers scaphandriers tombent du ciel. La température s'est brusquement adoucie et chaque matin la légèreté secoue sur nos toits ses cheveux d'ange. Contre les maléfices à quoi bon ce petit chien bleuâtre au corps pris dans un solénoïde de verre noir? Et pour une fois ne se peut-il que l'expression ***pour la vie*** déclenche une des aurores boréales dont sera fait le tapis de table du Jugement Dernier?

PRIVATE

Wearing a hooded beige cape, he frolics on the satin poster where two paradise feathers replace his spurs. She, with her special joints higher than breezes, divides the song of the radiant species. The hawthorn grows over what's left of the bleeding motor: then the first deepsea divers fall from the sky. The temperature has suddenly grown milder and every morning nimbleness shakes out its angel hair on our roofs. Against evil spells, what good is this little bluish dog with its body trapped in a solenoid of black glass? Just once can't the expression *for life* trigger one of the aurora borealises they'll use to make the tablecloth of the Last Judgment?

IL N'Y A PAS A SORTIR DE LA

A Paul Éluard

Liberté couleur d'homme
Quelles bouches voleront en éclats
Tuiles
Sous la poussée de cette végétation monstrueuse

Le soleil chien couchant
Abandonne le perron d'un riche hôtel particulier

Lente poitrine bleue où bat le cœur du temps

Une jeune fille nue aux bras d'un danseur beau et cuirassé comme saint Georges
Mais ceci est beaucoup plus tard
Faibles Atlantes

★

Rivière d'étoiles
Qui entraînes les signes de ponctuation de mon poème et de ceux de mes amis

Il ne faut pas oublier que cette liberté et toi je vous ai tirées à la courte paille
Si c'est elle que j'ai conquise
Quelle autre que vous arrive en glissant le long d'une corde de givre

THERE'S NO WAY OUT OF HERE

To Paul Éluard

Liberty the human color
What mouths will fly to pieces
Roof tiles
Under the thrust of this monstrous vegetation

The sun a setter dog
Leaves the stoop of a fancy town house

Slow blue chest where the heart of time beats
A naked girl in the arms of a male dancer handsome and armored like Saint George
But this comes much later on
Weak Atlantes

★

Stream of stars
Who washes away the punctuation marks of my poem and those of my friends
You mustn't forget that in drawing lots I won liberty and you
If she's what I won
Who else but you comes here by sliding down a rope of frost

Cet explorateur aux prises avec les fourmis rouges de son propre sang

C'est jusqu'à la fin le même mois de l'année
Perspective qui permet de juger si l'on a affaire à des âmes ou non
19... Un lieutenant d'artillerie s'attend dans une traînée de poudre

★

Aussi bien le premier venu
Penché sur l'ovale du désir intérieur
Dénombre ces buissons d'après le ver luisant
Selon que vous étendrez la main pour faire l'arbre ou avant de faire l'amour

Comme chacun sait

Dans l'autre monde qui n'existera pas
Je te vois blanc et élégant
Les cheveux des femmes ont l'odeur de la feuille d'acanthe
0 vitres superposées de la pensée
Dans la terre de verre s'agitent les squelettes de verre

★

Tout le monde a entendu parler du Radeau de la Méduse
Et peut à la rigueur concevoir un équivalent de ce radeau dans le ciel

That explorer grappling with the red ants of his own blood
Right to the end it's the same month of the year
Perspective which allows us to judge if we have to deal with souls or not
19... An artillery lieutenant is waiting in a trail of gunpowder

★

For that matter the first one to come along
Bent over the oval of inner desire
Counts those bushes by the glowworm
Depending on whether you stretch your hand for a handstand or before making love

As everyone knows

In the other world that won't exist
I see you white and elegant
Women's hair smells like acanthus leaves
O superimposed windowpanes of thought
In glass earth glass skeletons are stirring

★

Everyone's heard of the Raft of the Medusa
And could if it came down to it conceive of an equivalent of that raft in the sky

LE BUVARD DE CENDRE

A Robert Desnos

Les oiseaux s'ennuieront

Si j'avais oublié quelque chose

Sonnez la cloche de ces sorties d'école dans la mer
Ce que nous appellerons la bourrache pensive

On commence par donner la solution du concours
A savoir combien de larmes peuvent tenir dans une main de femme
1° aussi petite que possible
2° dans une main moyenne

Tandis que je froisse ce journal étoilé
Et que les chairs éternelles entrées une fois pour toutes en possession du sommet des montagnes
J'habite sauvagement une petite maison du Vaucluse

Cœur lettre de cachet

BLOTTER OF ASH

To Robert Desnos

The birds will be bored

If I'd forgotten something

Ring the bell of those last schooldays in the sea
What we'll call the pensive borage

We'll begin by giving the answer to the contest
About how many tears can fit in a woman's hand

1. that's as small as can be
2. in an average hand

While I crumple this starry newspaper
And while the eternal flesh which has once and for all come into
possession of the mountaintops
I dwell savagely in a little house in the Vaucluse

My heart a lettre de cachet

AU REGARD DES DIVINITES

A Louis Aragon

« Un peu avant minuit près du débarcadère.
« Si une femme échevelée te suit n'y prends pas garde.
« C'est l'azur. Tu n'as rien à craindre de l'azur.
« Il y aura un grand vase blond dans un arbre.
« Le clocher du village des couleurs fondues
« Te servira de point de repère. Prends ton temps,
« Souviens-toi. Le geyser brun qui lance au ciel les
pousses de fougère
« Te salue. »
La lettre cachetée aux trois coins d'un
poisson
Passait maintenant dans la lumière des faubourgs
Comme une enseigne de dompteur.
Au demeurant
La belle, la victime, celle qu'on appelait
Dans le quartier la petite pyramide de réséda
Décousait pour elle seule un nuage pareil
A un sachet de pitié.
Plus tard l'armure blanche
Qui vaquait aux soins domestiques et autres
En prenant plus fort à son aise que jamais,
L'enfant à la coquille, celui qui devait être...
Mais silence.
Un brasier déjà donnait prise

IN THE EYES OF THE GODS

To Louis Aragon

"A little before midnight down by the docks.
If a disheveled woman follows you don't pay any attention.
It's the azure. You don't have to be afraid of the azure.
There'll be a large blond vase in a tree.
The bell tower of the town with blended colors
Will be your reference point. Take your time,
Remember. The brown geyser hurling fern shoots into the sky
Salutes you."

The letter sealed with a fish's three corners
Was now passing by in the light of the suburbs
Like an animal tamer's sign.
All the same,
The beautiful woman, the victim, the one known
In the neighborhood as the little reseda pyramid
Unstitched just for herself a cloud like
A sachet of pity.
Later the white armor
That used to take care of household and other chores
Taking it easy now more than ever,
The child with the seashell, the one supposed to be...
But shh.
A brazier was already baring

En son sein à un ravissant roman de cape
Et d'épée.
                    Sur le pont, à la même heure.
Ainsi la rosée à tête de chatte se berçait.
La nuit, — et les illusions seraient perdues.

Voici les Pères blancs qui reviennent de vêpres
Avec l'immense clé pendue au-dessus d'eux.
Voici les hérauts gris; enfin voici sa lettre
Ou sa lèvre : mon cœur est un coucou pour Dieu.

Mais le temps qu'elle parle, il ne reste qu'un mur
Battant dans un tombeau comme une voile bise.
L'éternité recherche une montre-bracelet
Un peu avant minuit près du débarcadère.

Its breast to a delightful cloak-
And-dagger story.
                                        On the bridge, at the same time,
Like so the cat-headed dew rocked back and forth.
Night,—and their illusions would be lost.

Here are the white Fathers coming back from vespers
With the immense key hanging above them.
Here are the gray heralds; finally here's her letter
Or her lip: my heart is a cuckoo for God.

But by the time she speaks, nothing's left except a wall
Flapping inside a tomb like an unbleached sail.
Eternity searches for a wristwatch
A little before midnight down by the docks.

TOUT PARADIS N'EST PAS PERDU

A Man Ray

Les coqs de roche passent dans le cristal
Ils défendent la rosée à coups de crête
Alors la devise charmante de l'éclair
Descend sur la bannière des ruines
Le sable n'est plus qu'une horloge phosphorescente
Qui dit minuit
Par les bras d'une femme oubliée
Point de refuge tournant dans la campagne
Dressée aux approches et aux reculs célestes
C'est ici
Les tempes bleues et dures de la villa baignent dans
la nuit qui décalque mes images
Chevelures chevelures
Le mal prend des forces tout près
Seulement voudra-t-il de nous

NOT ALL OF PARADISE IS LOST

To Man Ray

Weathercocks turn into crystal
They protect the dew with blows from their crests
Then that charming emblem the thunderbolt
Descends on the banner of the ruins
The sand is nothing but a phosphorescent clock
That says midnight
With the arms of a forgotten woman
No place of refuge turning in the countryside
Erected where the heavens advance and retreat
It's here
The harsh blue temples of the villa's head bathe in the night that traces my images
Hair hair
Evil grows stronger nearby
But what does it want from us

MA MORT PAR ROBERT DESNOS

Le jeudi suivant les académiciens occupés au
dictionnaire
L'œil vitreux des hirondelles de bas étage
Un jardin aux parterres d'explosions

C'était à la veille de***
Sur r écorce des marronniers les mots A suivre
On parait on se contentait de parer

Jamais la religion au secours de l'opinion
Ne s'était à ce point commise
Dans une cabine de bains
J'entrais avec la Vierge en personne

Sachez que le baril de poudre Le Penseur
Durant la nuit avait été hissé
Au sommet de la Trinité

Je reviens au même

Les individus sont des crics
Et je me balance sans cesse en arrière de moi-même
Pareil à la suspension de la peur

Ma course est celle de cinq jockeys
Le premier bute sur ma tête
Loin des tribunes

MY DEATH BY ROBERT DESNOS

The following Thursday the academicians busy with the dictionary
The glassy eye of the low-life swallows
A garden with explosions for flower beds

It was the night before ***
On the chestnut trees' bark the words To be continued
We pushed it away we were happy to push it away

Never had religion so committed itself
To come to the aid of opinion
In a cabana
I came in with the Virgin in person

Bear in mind that the powder keg The Thinker
Had been hoisted during the night
To Trinity's topmost height

That's what I add up to

Individuals are car jacks
And I teeter endlessly behind myself
Like the postponement of fear

My race has five jockeys
The first butts my head
Far from the grandstands

Là où les haies sont remplacées par des avalanches
Le second part seul

Le quatrième pousse à la consommation des noix de coco en guise de cierges
Mais le sixième virtuel
Dans la glace de mes jours impossibles
Ressemble à une patte de renard
Je m'arrache difficilement à la contemplation des sourcils
Au vert des sangs et des mines
A l'apparence humaine qui dissémine

Plus j'aime plus je suis aimé des bois où le cerf dans la serpolet
Se signe à connaître que veux-tu

Descendre estimer mourir

Puis l'élément femelle croix des inquisiteurs

There where the jumps are replaced by avalanches
The second goes off alone

The fourth one pushes for coconuts to be used instead of candles
But the sixth virtual image
In the mirror of my impossible days
Resembles a fox's paw
With difficulty I tear myself away from the contemplation of eyebrows

From the green of bloods and gestures
From the human form which disseminates itself

The more I love the more I'm loved by the woods where the stag in the wild thyme
Crosses itself to know what do you want

Going down valuing dying

Then the female element the inquisitors' cross

PLUTOT LA VIE

Plutôt la vie que ces prismes sans épaisseur même si les couleurs sont plus pures
Plutôt que cette heure toujours couverte que ces terribles voitures de flammes froides
Que ces pierres blettes
Plutôt ce cœur à cran d'arrêt
Que cette mare aux murmures
Et que cette étoffe blanche qui chante à la fois dans l'air et dans la terre
Que cette bénédiction nuptiale qui joint mon front à celui de la vanité totale
Plutôt la vie

Plutôt la vie avec ses draps conjuratoires
Ses cicatrices d'évasions
Plutôt la vie plutôt cette rosace sur ma tombe
La vie de la présence rien que de la présence
Où une voix dit Es-tu là où une autre répond Es-tu là
Je n'y suis guère hélas
Et pourtant quand nous ferions le jeu de ce que nous faisons mourir
Plutôt la vie

Plutôt la vie plutôt la vie Enfance vénérable
Le ruban qui part d'un fakir
Ressemble à la glissière du monde

CHOOSE LIFE

Choose life instead of those prisms with no depth even if their colors
are purer

Instead of this hour always hidden instead of these terrible vehicles
of cold flame
Instead of these over-ripe stones
Choose this heart with its safety catch
Instead of that murmuring pool
And that white fabric singing in the air and the earth at the same time
Instead of that marriage blessing joining my forehead to total vanity's
Choose life

Choose life with its conspiratorial sheets
Its scars from escapes
Choose life choose that rose window on my tomb
The life of being here nothing but being here
Where one voice says Are you there where another answers Are you
there
I'm hardly here at all alas
And even when we might be making fun of what we kill
Choose life

Choose life choose life venerable Childhood
The ribbon coming out of a fakir
Resembles the playground of the world

Le soleil a beau n'être qu'une épave
Pour peu que le corps de la femme lui ressemble
Tu songes en contemplant la trajectoire tout du long
Ou seulement en fermant les yeux sur l'orage adorable
qui a nom ta main
Plutôt la vie

Plutôt la vie avec ses salons d'attente
Lorsqu'on sait qu'on ne sera jamais introduit
Plutôt la vie que ces établissements thermaux
Où le service est fait par des colliers
Plutôt la vie défavorable et longue
Quand les livres se refermeraient ici sur des rayons
moins doux
Et quand là-bas il ferait mieux que meilleur il ferait
libre oui
Plutôt la vie

Plutôt la vie comme fond de dédain
A cette tête suffisamment belle
Comme l'antidote de cette perfection qu'elle appelle et
qu'elle craint
La vie le fard de Dieu
La vie comme un passeport vierge
Une petite ville comme Pont-à-Mousson
Et comme tout s'est déjà dit
Plutôt la vie

Though the sun is only a shipwreck
Insofar as a woman's body resembles it
You dream contemplating the whole length of its trajectory
Or only while closing your eyes on the adorable storm named your hand
Choose life

Choose life with its waiting rooms
When you know you'll never be shown in
Choose life instead of those health spas
Where you're served by drudges
Choose life unfavorable and long
When the books close again here on less gentle shelves
And when over there the weather would be better than better it would be free yes
Choose life

Choose life as the pit of scorn
With that head beautiful enough
Like the antidote to that perfection it summons and it fears
Life the makeup on God's face
Life like a virgin passport
A little town like Pont-à-Mousson
And since everything's already been said
Choose life instead

SILHOUETTE DE PAILLE

A Max Ernst

Donnez-moi des bijoux de noyées
Deux crèches
Une prêle et une marotte de modiste
Ensuite pardonnez-moi
Je n'ai pas le temps de respirer
Je suis un sort
La construction solaire m'a retenu jusqu'ici
Maintenant je n'ai plus qu'à laisser mourir
Demandez le barème
Au trot le poing fermé au-dessus de ma tête qui sonne
Un verre dans lequel s'ouvre un œil jaune
Le sentiment s'ouvre aussi
Mais les princesses s'accrochent à l'air pur
J'ai besoin d'orgueil
Et de quelques gouttes plates
Pour réchauffer la marmite de fleurs moisies
Au pied de l'escalier
Pensée divine au carreau étoilé de ciel bleu
L'expression des baigneuses c'est la mort du loup
Prenez-moi pour amie
L'amie des feux et des furets
Vous regarde à deux fois
Lissez vos peines
Ma rame de palissandre fait chanter vos cheveux

SILHOUETTE OF STRAW

To Max Ernst

Give me the jewels of drowned women
Two cribs
A scouring-rush and a tailor's dummy
Then forgive me
I don't have time to breathe
I'm a magic spell
Solar construction has detained me up to this point
Now I have nothing to do but let things die
Ask to see the schedule
And make it snappy the closed fist above my ringing head
A glass in which a yellow eye opens
Feelings open too
But princesses cling to pure air
I need pride
And some flat drops
To fertilize the pot of musty flowers
At the foot of the stairs
Divine thought in the starry pane of blue sky
The look on the women bathers is what kills the wolf
Let me be your girlfriend
The girlfriend of fires and ferrets
Thinks twice about you
Polish your sorrows
My Brazilian rosewood oar makes your hair sing

Un son palpable dessert la plage
Noire de la colère des seiches
Et rouge du côté du panonceau

A sound that you can touch empties the beach
Black from the anger of the cuttlefish
And red towards the sign

ISLE

DANS LA VALLÉE DU MONDE

A Joseph Delteil

Des animaux disjoints font le tour de la terre
Et demandent leur chemin à ma fantaisie
Qui elle-même fait le tour de la terre
Mais en sens inverse
Il en résulte de grands quiproquos
La Chine est frappée d'interdit
La péninsule balkanique est doublée par une partie du cortège
Au levant seize reptiles étoilés à partir d'un feu
Souterrain sont hissés au sommet d'un mât
Agitateur du ciel
L'approche des crinières blanches est saluée
Par les feuilles lancéolées
Dont le murmure accompagne ce poème
Au dire d'un chanteur
L'ombre des ailes des pattes des nageoires
Suffit à la renommée
L'azur condense les vapeurs précieuses
Les singes marins
Suspendus aux arbres de corail
Et le rossignol qui vit dans les épaves
Montrent le bois injecté de roses et de cocaïne
Les marches d'ambre
Qui mènent au trône des pensées

IN THE VALLEY OF THE WORLD

To Joseph Delteil

Some disjointed animals are travelling around the world
And ask directions of my imagination
Which itself is going around the world
But in the opposite direction
Great misunderstandings result from this
China is placed under interdict
The Balkan Peninsula is doubled by one part of the procession
In the Levant no sooner do sixteen starry reptiles get to an underground
Fire than they're hoisted to the top of a mast
Stirrer of the sky
The approach of white manes is greeted
By lanceolate leaves
Whose murmur accompanies this poem
According to a singer's statement
The shadow of wings of paws of fins
Lives up to its reputation
The azure condenses precious vapors
Sea monkeys
Hanging from coral trees
And the nightingale that lives in shipwrecks
Point out wood injected with roses and cocaine
The amber steps
Leading to the throne of thoughts

Laissent couler le sang prismatique
Les oreilles des éléphants qu'on prenait pour des pierres tombales
Dans la vallée du monde
Battent la mesure des siècles
Plus près les femmes par-dessus les villes de chasubles et de cerises
Les femmes poudrées par les fleurs
Les femmes dont le troupeau est conduit par les animaux fabuleux
Accusent de rigueur le principe
Qui assimile les plantes spectrales
L'amour à cinq branches l'hystérie flocon des appartements
A la mort la petite mort l'héliotropisme

Let prismatic blood flow
The ears of elephants mistaken for tombstones
In the valley of the world
Beat time with the centuries
A little nearer the women above the cities of chasubles and cherries
The women powdered by flowers
The women whose flock is led by imaginary animals
Accuse of undue severity the principle
That assimilates spectral plants
Love with five branches hysteria flake of apartments
Into death the little death the heliotropism

MILLE ET MILLE FOIS

A Francis Picabia

Sous le couvert des pas qui regagnent le soir une tour habitée par des signes mystérieux au nombre de onze
La neige que je prends dans la main et qui fond
Cette neige que j'adore fait des rêves et je suis un de ces rêves
Moi qui n'accorde au jour et à la nuit que la stricte jeunesse nécessaire
Ce sont deux jardins dans lesquels se promènent mes mains qui n'ont rien à faire
Et pendant que les onze signes se reposent
Je prends part à l'amour qui est une mécanique de cuivre et d'argent dans la haie
Je suis un des rouages les plus délicats de l'amour terrestre
Et l'amour terrestre cache les autres amours
A la façon des signes qui me cachent l'esprit
Un coup de couteau perdu siffle à l'oreille du promeneur
J'ai défait le ciel comme un lit merveilleux
Mon bras pend du ciel avec un chapelet d'étoiles
Qui descend de jour en jour
Et dont le premier grain va disparaître dans la mer
A la place de mes couleurs vivantes
Il n'y aura bientôt plus que de la neige sur la mer

A THOUSAND THOUSAND TIMES

To Francis Picabia

Under cover of footsteps returning at evening to a tower inhabited
by mysterious symbols eleven in number
The snow that melts as I grasp it in my hand
This snow I love has dreams and I am one of those dreams
I who grant to day and night only as much youth as they need
They are two gardens where my hands walk with nothing to do
And while the eleven symbols rest
I share a love that is a copper and silver mechanism in the hedges
I'm one of the most delicate gears in earthly love
And earthly love hides the other loves
The way the symbols hide the mind from me
A lost stab whizzes past the ear of a man walking
I've stripped the sky like a marvelous bed
My arm hangs from the sky with a rosary of stars
Descending day by day
Whose first bead will disappear into the sea
Instead of my vivid colors
Soon there won't be anything but snow on the sea

Les signes apparaissent à la porte
Ils sont de onze couleurs différentes et leurs dimensions respectives vous feraient mourir de pitié
L'un d'eux est obligé de se baisser et de se croiser les bras pour entrer dans la tour
J'entends l'autre qui brûle dans une région prospère
Et celui-ci à cheval sur l'industrie la rare industrie montagneuse
Pareille à l'onagre qui se nourrit de truites
Les cheveux les longs cheveux pommelés
Caractérisent le signe qui porte le bouclier doublement ogival
Il faut se méfier de l'idée que roulent les torrents
Ma construction ma belle construction page à page
Maison insensément vitrée à ciel ouvert à sol ouvert
C'est une faille dans le roc suspendu par des anneaux à la tringle du monde
C'est un rideau métallique qui se baisse sur des inscriptions divines
Que vous ne savez pas lire
Les signes n'ont jamais affecté que moi
Je prends naissance dans le désordre infini des prières
Je vis et je meurs d'un bout à l'autre de cette ligne
Cette ligne étrangement mesurée qui relie mon cœur à l'appui de votre fenêtre
Je corresponds par elle avec tous les prisonniers du monde

The symbols appear at the door
They are eleven different colors and their respective dimensions would make you die of pity
One of them has to bend down and cross its arms to enter the tower
I hear another one on fire in a prosperous region
And this one on horseback riding industry a rare example of mountainous industry
Like the wild donkey that feeds on trout
The hair the long dappled hair
Characterizes the symbol wearing the doubly ogival buckler
Beware of the idea rolled along by mountain streams
My construction my beautiful construction page by page
House insanely glazed in the wide-open sky the wide-open earth
It's a fault in the rock suspended by rings from the curtain rod of the world
It's a metallic curtain that comes down on divine inscriptions
That you don't know how to read
The symbols have never affected anyone but me
I am born in the infinite disorder of prayers
I live and die from one end of this line to the other
That strangely measured line that connects my heart to the ledge of your window
Through it I communicate with all the prisoners in the world

L'AIGRETTE

A Marcel Noll

Si seulement il faisait du soleil cette nuit
Si dans le fond de l'Opéra deux seins miroitants et clairs
Composaient pour le mot amour la plus merveilleuse lettrine vivante
Si le pavé de bois s'entrouvrait sur la cime des montagnes
Si l'hermine regardait d'un air suppliant
Le prêtre à bandeaux rouges
Qui revient du bagne en comptant les voitures fermées
Si l'écho luxueux des rivières que je tourmente
Ne jetait que mon corps aux herbes de Paris
Que ne grêle-t-il à l'intérieur des magasins de bijouterie
Au moins le printemps ne me ferait plus peur
Si seulement j'étais une racine de l'arbre du ciel
Enfin le bien dans la canne à sucre de l'air
Si l'on faisait la courte échelle aux femmes
Que vois-tu belle silencieuse
Sous l'arc de triomphe du Carrousel
Si le plaisir dirigeait sous l'aspect d'une passante éternelle
Les Chambres n'étant plus sillonnées que par l'œillade violette des promenoirs

THE EGRET

To Marcel Noll

If only the sun were shining tonight
If way in the back of the Paris Opera House two bright shimmering breasts
Composed the most marvelous living ornamental letter to begin the word Amour
If the wooden street opened onto the mountains' summit
If the ermine looked imploringly
At the priest with red bandages
Who's coming back from the prison counting locked cars
If the luxurious echo of the rivers I lash
Hurled only my body on the Paris lawns
If only it would rain in jewelry stores
At least spring wouldn't scare me any more
If only I were a root of the gingko tree
In short whatever's good in the sugar cane of the air
If women were given a boost
Beautiful silent one what do you see
Under the Arc de Triomphe du Carrousel
If with the appearance of an eternal female passerby pleasure controlled
The Legislature no longer being furrowed except by the violet glance of the lobby

Que ne donnerais-je pour qu'un bras de la Seine se glissât sous le matin
Qui est de toute façon perdu
Je ne suis pas résigné non plus aux salles caressantes
Où sonne le téléphone des amendes du soir
En partant j'ai mis le feu à une mèche de cheveux qui est celle d'une bombe
Et la mèche de cheveux creuse un tunnel sous Paris
Si seulement mon train entrait dans ce tunnel

What I wouldn't give to have had an arm of the Seine slip under the morning
Which in any case is lost
Nor am I resigned to endearing rooms
Where the telephone of last night's penance is ringing
As I leave I set fire to a lock of hair that's the fuse of a bomb
And that bit of hair drills a tunnel under Paris
If only my train were entering that tunnel

LIGNE BRISÉE

A Raymond Roussel

Nous le pain sec et l'eau dans les prisons du ciel
Nous les pavés de l'amour tous les signaux interrompus
Qui personnifions les grâces de ce poème
Rien ne nous exprime au-delà de la mort
A cette heure où la nuit pour sortir met ses bottines
vernies
Nous prenons le temps comme il vient
Comme un mur mitoyen à celui de nos prisons
Les araignées font entrer le bateau dans la rade
Il n'y a qu'à toucher il n'y a rien à voir
Plus tard vous apprendrez qui nous sommes
Nos travaux sont encore bien défendus
Mais c'est l'aube de la dernière côte le temps se gâte
Bientôt nous porterons ailleurs notre luxe
embarrassant
Nous porterons ailleurs le luxe de la peste
Nous un peu de gelée blanche sur les fagots humains
Et c'est tout
L'eau-de-vie panse les blessures dans un caveau par le
soupirail duquel on aperçoit une route bordée de
grandes patiences vides
Ne demandez pas où vous êtes
Nous le pain sec et l'eau dans les prisons du ciel
Le jeu de cartes à la belle étoile

BROKEN LINE

To Raymond Roussel

We are the bread and water in the prisons of the sky
We are the pavements of love all the broken traffic lights
That personify the charms of this poem
Nothing speaks for us after death
In that hour when night puts on its shiny ankle-boots to go out
We take the weather as it comes
Like a wall adjoining one of our prisons
The spidery grapnels haul the boat into the roadstead
All you can do is touch there's nothing to see
Later on you'll find out who we are
The things we make are still totally banned
But the last coast is dawning the weather's breaking up
Soon we'll bring our embarrassing abundance somewhere else
We'll bring the abundance of our plague somewhere else
We are a touch of white frost on the bundle of human firewood
And that's all
Brandy dresses the wounds in a cellar bar through whose vent a
road can be seen bordered by
large solitary patience plants
Don't ask where you are
We are the bread and water in the prisons of the sky
The card game under the stars

Nous soulevons à peine un coin du voile
Le raccommodeur de faïence travaille sur une échelle
Il parait jeune en dépit de la concession
Nous portons son deuil en jaune
Le pacte n'est pas encore signé
Les sœurs de charité provoquent
A l'horizon des fuites
Peut-être pallions-nous à la fois le mal et le bien
C'est ainsi que la volonté des rêves se fait
Gens qui pourriez
Nos rigueurs se perdent dans le regret des émiettements
Nous sommes les vedettes de la séduction plus terrible
Le croc du chiffonnier Matin sur les bardes fleuries
Nous jette à la fureur des trésors aux dents longues
N'ajoutez rien à la honte de votre propre pardon
C'est assez que d'armer pour une fin sans fond
Vos yeux de ces larmes ridicules qui nous soulagent
Le ventre des mots est doré ce soir et rien n'est plus en vain

We can barely lift a corner of the veil
The man mending china works on a ladder
He seems young in spite of the concessions he's made
We mourn him by wearing yellow
The agreement hasn't been signed yet
The Sisters of Charity provoke
An exodus to the horizon
Maybe we conceal evil and good at the same time
That's how the will of dreams develops
Oh people Who could do it
Our struggles are lost amidst regret for our crumblings
We are the movie stars of the most terrible seduction
The hook of ragman morning on flower piles of old clothes
Throws us to the rage of sharp-toothed treasures
Don't add a thing to the shame of your own pardon
It's hard enough to arm yourself for an ending that never comes
Your eyes with those ridiculous tears assuaging us
The belly of words is gilded this evening and nothing's in vain any more

TOURNESOL

A Pierre Reverdy

La voyageuse qui traversa les Halles à la tombée de l'été
Marchait sur la pointe des pieds
Le désespoir roulait au ciel ses grands arums si beaux
Et dans le sac à main il y avait mon rêve ce flacon de sels
Que seule a respirés la marraine de Dieu
Les torpeurs se déployaient comme la buée
Au Chien qui fume
Où venaient d'entrer le pour et le contre
La jeune femme ne pouvait être vue d'eux que mal et de biais
Avais-je affaire à l'ambassadrice du salpêtre
Ou de la courbe blanche sur fond noir que nous appelons pensée
Le bal des innocents battait son plein
Les lampions prenaient feu lentement dans les marronniers
La dame sans ombre s'agenouilla sur le Pont au Change
Rue Gît-le-Cœur les timbres n'étaient plus les mêmes
Les promesses des nuits étaient enfin tenues
Les pigeons voyageurs les baisers de secours
Se joignaient aux seins de la belle inconnue
Dardés sous le crêpe des significations parfaites

SUNFLOWER

To Pierre Reverdy

The traveler who passed through Les Halles as summer fell
Walked on her tiptoes
Despair rolled its big beautiful arums toward the sky
And in her handbag was my dream that flask of smelling-salts
That only God's godmother has inhaled
The torpors spread like steam
At the Smoking Dog
Where the pros and cons had just walked in
They could hardly see her and then only from a bad angle
Had I business with the ambassadress of saltpeter
Or of the white curve on the black background we call thought
The Ball of the Innocents was in full swing
Chinese lanterns slowly caught fire in the chestnut trees
The lady without a shadow knelt on the Pont au Change
Rue Gît-le-Coeur the bells weren't the same any more
The nights' promises were finally kept
The homing pigeons the emergency kisses
Merged at the beautiful unknown woman's breasts
That flashed beneath the crape of perfect meanings

Une ferme prospérait en plein Paris
Et ses fenêtres donnaient sur la voie lactée
Mais personne ne l'habitait encore à cause des survenants
Des survenants qu'on sait plus dévoués que les revenants
Les uns comme cette femme ont l'air de nager
Et dans l'amour il entre un peu de leur substance
Elle les intériorise
Je ne suis le jouet d'aucune puissance sensorielle
Et pourtant le grillon qui chantait dans les cheveux de cendre
Un soir près la statue d'Étienne Marcel
M'a jeté un coup d'œil d'intelligence
André Breton a-t-il dit passe

A farm prospered in the middle of Paris
And its windows looked on the Milky Way
But no one lived there yet because of the people who stumbled
upon this neighborhood
Who everyone knows are more devoted than the ghosts who
stumble around this neighborhood
The ones like this woman who seem to be swimming
And a touch of their substance enters into love
She interiorizes them
I'm not the plaything of any sensorial power
And yet the cricket that sang in the ashen hair
One evening near the statue of Étienne Marcel
Aimed a nod of recognition at me
André Breton it said you may pass

LE SOLEIL EN LAISSE

A Pablo Picasso

Le grand frigorifique blanc dans la nuit des temps
Qui distribue les frissons à la ville
Chante pour lui seul
Et le fond de sa chanson ressemble à la nuit
Qui fait bien ce qu'elle fait et pleure de le savoir
Une nuit où j'étais de quart sur un volcan
J'ouvris sans bruit la porte d'une cabine et me jetai aux pieds de la lenteur
Tant je la trouvai belle et prête à m'obéir
Ce n'était qu'un rayon de la roue voilée
Au passage des morts elle s'appuyait sur moi
Jamais les vins braisés ne nous éclairèrent
Mon amie était trop loin des aurores qui font cercle autour d'une lampe arctique
Au temps de ma millième jeunesse
J'ai charmé cette torpille qui brille
Nous regardons l'incroyable et nous y croyons malgré nous
Comme je pris un jour la femme que j'aimais
Nous rendons les lumières heureuses
Elles se piquent à la cuisse devant moi
Posséder est un trèfle auquel j'ai ajouté artificiellement la quatrième feuille
Les canicules me frôlent

THE SUN ON A LEASH

To Pablo Picasso

The big white cold storage room in the mists of time
That sends out shivers to the city
Sings to itself
And the musical background of its song resembles night
Which does what it does well and weeps because it knows it
One night when I was keeping watch over a volcano
Without a sound I opened the door of a cabin and threw myself at the feet of slowness
I found it that beautiful and that ready to obey me
It was only a spoke of a bent wheel
When the dead passed by it leaned against me
Braised wines never lit the way for us
My girlfriend was too far from the dawns that make a ring around an arctic lamp
At the time of my thousandth childhood
I charmed that shining torpedo fish
We see the unbelievable and we believe it in spite of ourselves
The way one day I took the woman I loved
We make lights happy
They sting themselves in the thigh in front of me
Possession is a clover to which I've artificially added the fourth leaf
The dog days brush against me

Comme les oiseaux qui tombent
Sous l'ombre il y a une lumière et sous cette lumière
il y a deux ombres
Le fumeur met la dernière main à son travail
Il cherche l'unité de lui-même avec le paysage
Il est un des frissons du grand frigorifique

Like falling birds
Beneath the shadow there's a light and beneath that light there are two shadows
The smoker puts the finishing touches on his work
He's looking for the union of himself and the landscape
He's one of the shivers of the big cold storage room

A RROSE SÉLAVY

« André Breton n'écrira plus. »
(Journal du Peuple — Avril 1923)

J'ai quitté mes effets,
mes beaux effets de neige!

TO RROSE SÉLAVY

"André Breton has given up writing."
(*Journal du Peuple*—April 1923)

I've left my effects behind,
my special snow effects!

L'UNION LIBRE

(1931)

FREE UNION

(1931)

Ma femme à la chevelure de feu de bois
Aux pensées d'éclairs de chaleur
A la taille de sablier
Ma femme à la taille de loutre entre les dents du tigre
Ma femme à la bouche de cocarde et de bouquet d'étoiles de dernière grandeur
Aux dents d'empreintes de souris blanche sur la terre blanche
A la langue d'ambre et de verre frottés
Ma femme à la langue d'hostie poignardée
A la langue de poupée qui ouvre et ferme les yeux
A la langue de pierre incroyable
Ma femme aux cils de bâtons d'écriture d'enfant
Aux sourcils de bord de nid d'hirondelle
Ma femme aux tempes d'ardoise de toit de serre
Et de buée aux vitres
Ma femme aux épaules de champagne
Et de fontaine à têtes de dauphins sous la glace
Ma femme aux poignets d'allumettes
Ma femme aux doigts de hasard et d'as de cœur
Aux doigts de foin coupé
Ma femme aux aisselles de martre et de fênes
De nuit de la Saint-Jean
De troène et de nid de scalares

My woman with her forest-fire hair
With her heat-lightning thoughts
With her hourglass waist
My woman with her otter waist in the tiger's mouth
My woman with her rosette mouth a bouquet of stars of the
  brightest magnitude
With her teeth of white mouse footprints on the white earth
With her tongue of polished amber and glass
My woman with her stabbed eucharist tongue
With her tongue of a doll that opens and closes its eyes
With her tongue of incredible stone
My woman with her eyelashes in a child's handwriting
With her eyebrows the edge of a swallow's nest
My woman with her temples of a greenhouse with a slate roof
And steam on the windowpanes
My woman with her shoulders of champagne
And a dolphin-headed fountain under ice
My woman with her matchstick wrists
My woman with her lucky fingers her acc of hearts fingers
With her fingers of new-mown hay
My woman with her armpits of marten and beechnuts
Of Midsummer Night
Of privet and angelfish nest

Aux bras d'écume de mer et d'écluse
Et de mélange du blé et du moulin
Ma femme aux jambes de fusée
Aux mouvements d'horlogerie et de désespoir
Ma femme aux mollets de moelle de sureau
Ma femme aux pieds d'initiales
Aux pieds de trousseaux de clés aux pieds de calfats
qui boivent
Ma femme au cou d'orge imperlé
Ma femme à la gorge de Val d'or
De rendez-vous dans le lit même du torrent
Aux seins de nuit
Ma femme aux seins de taupinière marine
Ma femme aux seins de creuset du rubis
Aux seins de spectre de la rose sous la rosée
Ma femme au ventre de dépliement d'éventail des jours
Au ventre de griffe géante
Ma femme au dos d'oiseau qui fuit vertical
Au dos de vif-argent
Au dos de lumière
A la nuque de pierre roulée et de craie mouillée
Et de chute d'un verre dans lequel on vient de boire
Ma femme aux hanches de nacelle
Aux hanches de lustre et de pennes de flèche
Et de tiges de plumes de paon blanc
De balance insensible
Ma femme aux fesses de grès et d'amiante

With her seafoam and floodgate arms
Arms that mingle the wheat and the mill
My woman with rocket legs
With her movements of clockwork and despair
My woman with her calves of elder tree pith
My woman with her feet of initials
With her feet of bunches of keys with her feet of weaverbirds
  taking a drink
My woman with her pearl barley neck
My woman with her Val d'or cleavage
Cleavage of a rendezvous in the very bed of the mountain
  stream
With her breasts of night
My woman with her undersea molehill breasts
My woman with her breasts of the crucible of rubies
With her breasts of the specter of the rose beneath the dew
My woman with her belly of the unfolding fan of days
With her giant claw belly
My woman with her back of a bird fleeing vertically
With her quicksilver back
With her back of light
With her nape of rolled stone and damp chalk
And a falling glass that's just been sipped
My woman with her hips like a canoe
With her hips of a chandelier and arrow feathers
And stems of white peacock plumes
Her hips an imperceptible pair of scales
My woman with her buttocks of sandstone and asbestos

Ma femme aux fesses de dos de cygne
Ma femme aux fesses de printemps
Au sexe de glaïeul
Ma femme au sexe de placer et d'ornithorynque
Ma femme au sexe d'algue et de bonbons anciens
Ma femme au sexe de miroir
Ma femme aux yeux pleins de larmes
Aux yeux de panoplie violette et d'aiguille aimantée
Ma femme aux yeux de savane
Ma femme aux yeux d'eau pour boire en prison
Ma femme aux yeux de bois toujours sous la hache
Aux yeux de niveau d'eau de niveau d'air de terre et de feu

My woman with the buttocks of a swan's back
My woman with her buttocks of springtime
With her gladiolus sex
My woman with her sex of placer and platypus
My woman with her sex of seaweed and old-fashioned candies
My woman with her mirror sex
My woman with her eyes full of tears
With her eyes of violet armor and a speedometer needle
My woman with her savannah eyes
My woman with her eyes of water to drink in prison
My woman with her eyes of forests forever beneath the axe
With her eyes of sea-level air-level earth and fire

LE REVOLVER À CHEVEUX BLANCS

(1932)

THE REVOLVER WITH WHITE HAIR

(1932)

IL Y AURA UNE FOIS

Imagination n'est pas don mais par excellence objet de conquête. « *Où,* se demande Huysmans, *dans quel temps, sous quelles latitudes, dans quels parages pouvait bien se lever ce palais immense, avec ses coupoles élancées dans la nue, ses colonnes phalliques, ses piliers émergés d'un pavé miroitant et dur ?* [1] » Manière toute lyrique, toute pessimiste, d'effacer au fur et à mesure tout ce qu'on pense, qui devrait être. Ce palais se *levait,* ce *palais*... Cet imparfait, cette splendeur inutile tendant à rejeter dans la gratuité quasi légendaire le besoin qu'on éprouve — ces *colonnes phalliques* — de se comporter, ne serait-ce qu'au point de vue sexuel, autrement qu'on se comporte, témoignent d'une lassitude coupable et d'un doute inadmissible touchant les forces réelles de l'esprit. La lamentable formule : « Mais ce n'était qu'un rêve », dont le croissant usage, entre autres cinématographique, n'a pas peu contribué à faire apparaître l'hypocrisie, a cessé depuis longtemps de mériter la discussion. Pourquoi ne pas le dire? Huysmans savait fort bien que telles visions qu'il avait — comme on peut les avoir : hors du temps — n'étaient pas moins destinées à entraîner le monde « en avant » qu' « en arrière ». A quoi bon, si ce n'est pour se mettre soi-même tristement à l'abri, à quoi bon accorder à ce qui,

1. *En rade.*

ONCE UPON A TIME TO COME

Imagination isn't a gift but par excellence an object of conquest. "*Where,*" wonders Huysmans, "*at what time, in what latitudes, in what waters could this immense palace actually rise, with its cupolas soaring to the clouds, its phallic columns, its pillars emerging from a hard, mirrory pavement?*"[1] A totally lyrical, totally pessimistic way of erasing everything one thinks, everything that should be, as fast as it happens. This palace was rising, palacing.... That imperfect tense, that useless splendor tending to reject with quasi-legendary gratuitousness the need one feels—those *phallic columns*—to behave, be it only from a sexual standpoint, otherwise than one behaves, bearing witness to a sinful lassitude and to an inadmissible doubt concerning the real powers of the mind. The lamentable formula: "But it was only a dream," whose growing usage, among others cinematographic, has contributed more than a little to the rise of hypocrisy, hasn't been worth discussing for a long time. Why not say it? Huysmans knew very well that the kinds of visions he had—as one can have them: outside time—were no less destined to carry the world "forward" than "backward." What good is it, unless one is going to gloomily retire to a safe refuge, what good is it to accord to that which, once again, should be, the frightening faculty of having been and no longer being!

---

1. *Becalmed.*

encore une fois, devrait être, l'effrayante faculté d'avoir été et de n'être plus ! Je sais l'objection : « Mais l'esprit bute à chaque pas contre des vestiges de temps et de lieux. Ses représentations sont esclaves de l'émotion plus ou moins grande que ces vestiges lui donnent. Fétichiste en diable ! Ce qu'il est convenu d'appeler le passé le prend, c'est indéniable, par son côté faible. Les nuits d'Antoine, le Mexique avant l'arrivée des Espagnols, une photographie d'inconnue datant du siècle dernier : vous, ici, là-bas, si vous bougez tâchez de ne pas faire trop de bruit. »

Mais où sont les neiges de demain? Je dis que l'imagination, à quoi qu'elle emprunte et — cela pour moi reste à démontrer — si véritablement elle *emprunte,* n'a pas à s'humilier devant la vie. Il y aura toujours, notamment, entre les idées dites reçues et les idées... qui sait, à faire recevoir, une différence susceptible de rendre l'imagination maîtresse de la situation de l'esprit. C'est tout le problème de la transformation de l'énergie qui se pose une fois de plus. Se défier comme on fait, outre mesure, de la vertu pratique de l'imagination, c'est vouloir se priver, coûte que coûte, des secours de l'électricité, dans l'espoir de ramener la houille blanche à sa conscience absurde de cascade.

L'imaginaire est ce qui tend à devenir réel.

A ce propos, je voudrais louer (je ne dis pas même acheter) une propriété dans les environs de Paris [1].

1. Il ne me manque que de l'argent.

I know the argument against this: "But at every step the mind stumbles into vestiges of certain times and places. Its images are slaves to the greater or lesser emotions that those vestiges gave it. Crazy fetishist! What we conveniently call the past catches it, undeniably, on its weak side. Saint Anthony's nights, Mexico before the arrival of the Spaniards, a photograph of an unknown woman dating from the last century: you over there, if you move try not to make too much noise."

But where are the snows of tomorrow? I say that the imagination, whatever it borrows from and—for me this remains to be proved—if it really does borrow, need not cringe before life. More particularly, there will always be, between the kinds of ideas we call cliché and ideas... who knows, which will become cliché, a difference susceptible to making the imagination mistress of the mind's estate. It's the whole question of the transformation of energy presenting itself once more. To mistrust as one does, beyond all bounds, the practical virtue of imagination, is to try to deprive oneself at all costs of the assistance of electricity in the hope of bringing hydroelectric power back to its absurd waterfall consciousness.

The imaginary is what tends to become real.

Apropos of which, I'd like to rent (I'll say nothing of buying) a property in the Paris suburbs.[1]

---

1. All I need is the money.

Rien de fabuleux. Seulement une trentaine de pièces, avec, autant que possible, de longs corridors très sombres ou que je me chargerais d'assombrir. Quatre ou cinq hectares de terrain boisé, tout autour. Quelques ruisseaux ou, de grande préférence, une ou deux mares, ne seraient pas mal vus. Je tiendrais, naturellement, à juger par moi-même de la sécurité du lieu (quand je parle de sécurité, les brigands me feront l'honneur de croire que ce n'est pas à eux que je pense). Qu'il soit possible à qui que ce soit — des gens *divers* à qui j'aurais donné rendez-vous — d'y entrer ou d'en sortir, de jour ou de nuit, sans que cela provoque d'esclandre. Toutes ces premières conditions, en somme, faciles à réaliser.

Un souterrain, à faire creuser ou non, pas plus difficile.

De l'extérieur : plutôt qu'un hôtel ou qu'une auberge, et aussi pour que ce soit tout à fait dépaysant, un relais. Mais de l'intérieur, comme on va voir, un relais dans lequel ceux qui, d'après moi, y ont droit, pourront toujours venir prendre des idées harassantes en échange d'idées harassées.

Il sera servi une pension *à temps* à... disons trois jeunes filles qui seront invitées à séjourner en cet endroit, ces jeunes filles étant les dernières à s'être signalées dans un scandale de maison hantée quelconque. On commencera par les mettre à l'aise en les persuadant qu'elles sont vraiment « chez elles ». En cas d'insuffisance notoire de leur part il sera pourvu aussitôt que possible

Nothing spectacular. Only about thirty rooms with, insofar as possible, long hallways, very dark, or which I'd make a point of darkening. Ten or twelve acres of wooded land all around it. A few streams or, preferably, one or two ponds would not be unwelcome. Naturally I'd want to make my own judgment about the security of the place (when I speak of security, thieves will do me the honor of believing that I'm not thinking of them). Let it be possible for whosoever it might be—the *various* people whom I'd agree to meet—to enter and leave there night or day without causing any scandal. In a word, all these preconditions easy to meet.

An underground passage, whether or not it needs to be dug, not presenting any further difficulties.

From the outside: rather than a hotel or an inn, and also so it makes you feel completely disoriented, a coach house. But from the inside, as you'll see, a coach house where those who, according to me, have the right to be there, could always come and hear tiring ideas in exchange for tired ideas.

Meals will be served regularly and *on time* to... let's say three girls who will be invited to spend time at this place, these girls being the most recent to have achieved renown in a scandal about some haunted house. We'd begin by putting them at ease by persuading them that they're really "at home." In case of any manifest deficiency on their part, replacements would be found for them as soon as possible. In case of an emergency, additional aid

à leur remplacement. En cas d'urgence il pourra leur être apporté une aide supplémentaire. (Il pourra même être fait appel à un jeune homme involontairement spécialisé dans ces sortes de questions, mais jamais à plus d'un à la fois). Il sera donné pour compagnes d'occasion à ces jeunes personnes quelques autres jeunes filles et quelques jeunes femmes en mesure de présenter, par ailleurs, des phénomènes médianimiques intéressants, ou qui se distingueront par l'étrangeté de leur esprit ou de leur beauté.

Par chambre, une grande horloge à verre noir sera dressée à sonner particulièrement *bien* minuit.

Il sera formellement interdit, sous peine d'expulsion immédiate et définitive, à qui que ce soit, et cela en dépit de toutes les provocations auxquelles il pourra se trouver en butte, d'accomplir, dans les limites de l'encerclement par le mur du parc, l'acte de l'amour.

Il n'y aura guère que de petites lampes d'étude, à abat-jour vert, très basses. Jour et nuit les persiennes demeurant fermées.

La chambre de réception, blanchie à la chaux, sera seule éclairée par un plafonnier invisible et ne comportera d'autre meuble, en plus de deux authentiques sièges mérovingiens, qu'une sellette sur laquelle sera posé le flacon de parfum noué d'une faveur pâle, à l'intérieur duquel baigne une rose décolorée avec sa tige et les feuilles également sans vie, qu'on peut voir aujourd'hui 9 juin, dans la vitrine sud de la pharmacie qui fait l'angle de la rue Lafayette et de la rue du faubourg Montmartre.

could be brought to them. (One might even call on a young man who involuntarily specializes in these kinds of things, though never on more than one young man at a time.) As occasional companions for these young persons we will provide several other girls and several young women who are incidentally in a position to present interesting mediumistic phenomena, or who are unusual for the strangeness of their minds or beauty.

In each room, a large clock made of black glass will be set to ring midnight *particularly* loud.

It will be strictly forbidden, on pain of immediate and permanent expulsion, for whomever it may be, despite all provocations to which one might be exposed, to perform, within the walls encircling the grounds, the act of love.

Hardly anything will be there except little desk lamps with green shades, very short. Day and night the blinds will remain closed.

The reception room, whitewashed, will be illuminated only by indirect light and will contain no other furniture than two authentic Merovingian chairs, except a stool on which will sit a perfume bottle, tied with a pale ribbon, inside of which steeps a discolored rose, its stems and leaves equally lifeless, which can be seen today, June 9th, in the south window of the pharmacy at the corner of the Rue Lafayette and the Rue du Faubourg Montmartre.

Et en cela finira l'arbitraire.

Mais les lâchers de papillons par la nature seront plus loin repris par l'homme et *commentés*. On verra bien, enfin, si les draps du lit sont faits pour servir d'enveloppe au corps de l'homme et de la femme (quelle adresse faut-il mettre?) ou si, de leur incompréhensible hauteur quand on les dresse, ils sont faits pour rendre imaginaire un corps imaginaire ou non, de manière à prouver que l'esprit humain, quoi qu'on dise, n'en est jamais *quitte pour la peur*. (On m'a raconté dernièrement cette charmante histoire de fantômes : deux hommes, conventionnellement déguisés, jouent à effrayer le monde ignare en faisant, plusieurs nuits consécutives, le tour d'un cimetière. Une nuit enfin un « esprit fort » les rejoint discrètement à un tournant et se mêle, de très près, de les suivre, non sans avoir pris soin de s'affubler comme eux. Conscience prise d'une telle présence dans leur dos, ils détalent. Je préfère ces deux premiers hommes à ce dernier.)

Un « puits mystérieux », pure et simple réplique de celui de Luna-Park, quoique à première vue moins *libre* mais plus divers, plus insistant et beaucoup plus joli.

Cinq chambres aux portes et fenêtres condamnées, d'un accès rendu pratiquement impossible, sans préjudice du serment prêté de ne pas chercher à y voir. Dans la première, je suppose, et la plus grande, auront été groupés les principaux spécimens de mannequins et de cires, ni les uns sur les autres, ni chacun dans un rôle, mais disposés

So much for the arbitrary.

But the flock of butterflies set loose by nature will be caught by man later on and *commented upon*. We shall see, in the end, if bedsheets are made to serve as an envelope for the bodies of men and women (what address would you put on them?) or if, with their incomprehensible height when spread out, they are made to turn imaginary a body which may or may not be imaginary so as to prove that the human mind, whatever one says about it, *escapes with something more than a fright*. (Recently I was told this charming ghost story: two men, dressed in the usual costumes, had fun scaring ignorant people several nights in a row by walking around a cemetery. Finally one night a "hardy soul" discreetly snuck up behind them at a bend and took it upon himself to follow them, not without having taken care to get himself up like them. Aware of a presence at their backs, they hightailed it out of there. I prefer the first two men to the third.)

A "wishing well," a pure and simple replica of the one at Luna Park, though on first sight less *free* but more diverse, more insistent and much prettier.

Five rooms, with their windows and doorways boarded up, access to them rendered almost impossible without compromising the oath taken to not try and look into them. In the first and, I suppose, the largest one, the finest specimens of mannequins and wax figures will have been gathered, not all piled together, nor with each one playing a part, but arranged in such a manner as they

de telle sorte qu'ils aient paru, avant murage, susciter au plus fort l'esprit d'abandon. Dans la seconde voisineront pêle-mêle des bagages excentriques, de grands tournesols et autres accessoires de cotillon de l'esprit ; elle sera tout entière tapissée de lettres d'amour. Dans la troisième, qu'on aura tenté de rendre la plus luxueuse de toutes les chambres d'enfant existantes, seul un berceau lacéré et orné en bonne place d'un poignard penchera, comme un navire en détresse, sur un plancher de vagues trop bleues. Il faut que je sois seul à savoir ce qui aura lieu dans la quatrième, afin qu'un seul autre homme sûr puisse connaître la véritable destination de la cinquième, sans posséder plus que moi ni qu'aucun autre la clé idéologique du tout [1]. Le pire est que la première chambre, de l'extérieur, ne sera en rien distinguable de la seconde ou de la cinquième. Les travaux d'aménagement seront conduits de manière à supprimer, a priori, toute possibilité d'indiscrétion.

Désireux de m'en tenir aujourd'hui à un schème simple, je ne m'étendrai pas inutilement sur l'ameublement des pièces occupables. Cela ne pourra être qu'absolument sévère bien entendu — le disparate extrême de l'ensemble devant répondre, bien plutôt qu'au caprice, à la nécessité. On peut, du reste, se fier à notre goût.

1. Un peu puéril ? Tant mieux.

might have appeared before the walling-in, to create the greatest spirit of abandon. In the second, eccentric suitcases, large sunflowers, and witty party favors will be thrown together side by side; its walls will be completely papered with love letters. In the third, which we will attempt to make the most luxurious nursery in the world, only a cradle, lacerated and decorated in the proper place by a dagger, will list, like a ship in distress, over a floor of waves that are too blue. Necessity dictates that I be the only one who knows what will take place in the fourth, and that just one trustworthy man should know the true purpose of the fifth, although he will not know more than me or anyone else about the ideological key to the whole.[1] The worst is that the first room, from the outside, will not be the slightest bit distinguishable from the second or fifth. The work of setting up the house will be carried out so as to eliminate, *a priori,* any possibility of indiscretion.

Desiring to limit myself today to a simple outline, I won't enlarge uselessly on the decorating scheme of the rooms that are to be occupied. This could only be, of course, absolutely austere—the disparate extremes within the whole corresponding much more to necessity than to capriciousness. As to the rest, one may trust our taste.

The most stringent regulations regarding physical hygiene will be scrupulously observed.

---

1. A little puerile? So much the better.

Les conditions de l'hygiène physique la plus exigeante seront minutieusement remplies.

Je ne sais pas encore, ma foi, si l'on confiera à la domesticité deux lévriers blancs ou deux bulls blancs de très haute race, ou si l'on pourra se passer de ces animaux.

. . . .

Ce qu'avant tout je veux défendre ici n'est que le principe d'une association dont les avantages seraient de placer l'esprit dans la position qui me parait poétiquement la plus favorable. Il ne saurait s'agir, pour l'instant d'entrer plus avant dans les secrets d'une telle communauté. Je répète qu'écrivant ces lignes, je fais momentanément abstraction de tout autre point de vue que le point de vue poétique, ce qui ne veut pas dire que j'accepte le moins du monde de passer pour me débattre dans l'utopie. Je me borne à indiquer une source de *mouvements* curieux, en grande partie imprévisibles, source qui, si l'on consentait une première fois à suivre sa pente — et je gage qu'on l'acceptera — serait, à ébranler des monts et des monts d'ennui, la promesse d'un magnifique torrent. On ne peut se défendre de penser ainsi et de prévoir, devant ces aveugles architectures d'aujourd'hui, mille fois plus stupides et plus révoltantes que celles d'autrefois. Comme on va pouvoir s'ennuyer là-dedans ! Ah! l'on est bien sûr que rien ne se passera. Mais si, tout à coup, un homme entendait, même en pareil domaine, que quelque chose se passât! S'il osait s'aventurer, seul ou presque, sur

Actually, I still don't know if we'll decide to keep on the premises two white greyhounds or two white terriers of very pure pedigree, or if we can get along without these animals.

. . . .

What, above all, I wish to defend here is only the guiding principle of a fellowship whose advantage would be to place the mind in a position that seems to me poetically the most favorable. The matter at hand, right now, is not to delve any deeper into the secrets of such a community. I repeat that, while writing these lines, I am momentarily leaving out of consideration all other points of view than the poetic, which doesn't in the least mean that I accept the judgment that I'm thrashing about in utopia. I'm content to point out a source of curious *movements*, to a large degree unforeseeable, a source which, once one consents to follow its direction—and I bet that it will be accepted—would be, for overturning mountains and mountains of boredom, the promise of a magnificent stream. One can't help but think this way and look ahead, faced with today's blind architecture, a thousand times more stupid and revolting than that of times gone by. How bored we'll be inside it! Ah! You can be certain nothing will happen there. But if, suddenly, a man heard, even in such a domain, that something had happened! If he dared to venture out, alone or almost so, over lands where chance has struck? If, his mind defogged of those stories which as children delighted

les terres foudroyées du hasard? Si, l'esprit désembrumé de ces contes qui, enfants, faisaient nos délices tout en commençant dans nos cœurs à creuser la déception, cet homme se risquait à arracher sa proie de mystère au passé? Si ce poète voulait pénétrer lui-même dans l'Antre? S'il était, lui, vraiment résolu à n'ouvrir la bouche que pour dire : « Il y aura une fois... »?

us while beginning to hollow out a place in our hearts for deception, that man would risk snatching out of the hands of the past its mysterious prey? If that poet himself wanted to penetrate the Lair? If he was, himself, truly resolved to open his mouth only to say: "Once upon a time to come..."?

LA MORT ROSE

Les pieuvres ailées guideront une dernière fois la barque dont les voiles sont faites de ce seul jour heure par heure
C'est la veillée unique après quoi tu sentiras monter dans tes cheveux le soleil blanc et noir
Des cachots suintera une liqueur plus forte que la mort
Quand on la contemple du haut d'un précipice
Les comètes s'appuieront tendrement aux forêts avant de les foudroyer
Et tout passera dans l'amour indivisible
Si jamais le motif des fleuves disparait
Avant qu'il fasse complètement nuit tu observeras
La grande pause de l'argent
Sur un pêcher en fleur apparaîtront les mains
Qui écrivirent ces vers et qui seront des fuseaux d'argent
Elles aussi et aussi des hirondelles d'argent sur le métier de la pluie
Tu verras l'horizon s'entrouvrir et c'en sera fini tout à coup du baiser de l'espace
Mais la peur n'existera déjà plus et les carreaux du ciel et de la mer
Voleront au vent plus fort que nous
Que ferai-je du tremblement de ta voix
Souris valseuse autour du seul lustre qui ne tombera pas

THE PINK DEATH

For one last time octopuses with wings will guide the boat
whose sails are made of just this day hour by hour
This is the one vigil after which you'll feel the black and
white sun rising in your hair
A liqueur stronger than death will ooze from dungeons
When seen from high on a cliff
Comets will lean tenderly against forests before blasting
them
And all shall pass into indivisible love
If the rivers' motive ever disappears
Before it's completely dark you'll notice
Silver take a long pause
On a blossoming peach tree the hands will appear
That wrote these lines hands that will be silver spindles
Those too and silver swallows too on the loom of the rain
You'll see the horizon half opening and suddenly it will
all be over with one kiss of space
But by then fear won't exist anymore and the window-
panes of the sky and of the sea
Will fly in a wind stronger than us
What am I to make of your trembling voice
Mouse waltzing around the only chandelier that won't fall

Treuil du temps
Je monterai les cœurs des hommes
Pour une suprême lapidation
Ma faim tournoiera comme un diamant trop taillé
Elle nattera les cheveux de son enfant le feu
Silence et vie
Mais les noms des amants seront oubliés
Comme l'adonide goutte de sang
Dans la lumière folle
Demain tu mentiras à ta propre jeunesse
A ta grande jeunesse luciole
Les échos mouleront seuls tous ces lieux qui furent
Et dans l'infinie végétation transparente
Tu te promèneras avec la vitesse
Qui commande aux bêtes des bois
Mon épave peut-être tu t'y égratigneras
Sans la voir comme on se jette sur une arme flottante
C'est que j'appartiendrai au vide semblable aux marches
D'un escalier dont le mouvement s'appelle *bien en peine*
A toi les parfums dès lors les parfums défendus
L'angélique
Sous la mousse creuse et sous tes pas qui n'en sont pas
Mes rêves seront formels et vains comme le bruit de paupières de l'eau dans l'ombre

Winch of time
I'll haul up the hearts of men
For a supreme lapidation
My hunger will spin like a diamond cut too many times
It will braid the hair of fire its child
Silence and life
But the names of lovers will be forgotten
Like the adonis a drop of blood
In the mad light
Tomorrow you'll lie to the days when you were young
To the great firefly days when you were young
Only echoes will make the mold of all those places that used to be
And in the infinite transparent vegetation
You'll walk with the speed
That controls the beasts of the jungle
Maybe you'll bump into my shipwreck there
Without seeing it the way someone dives onto a floating weapon
It's just that I'll belong to the emptiness that's like the steps
Of a stairway whose traffic is called *totally at a loss*
Your perfumes forbidden perfumes since then
The angelica
Under the sunken moss and under your feet that aren't there
My dreams will be formal and vain like the sound of the water's eyelids in the shade

Je m'introduirai dans les tiens pour y sonder la profondeur
    de tes larmes
Mes appels te laisseront doucement incertaine
Et dans le train fait de tortues de glace
Tu n'auras pas à tirer le signal d'alarme
Tu arriveras seule sur cette plage perdue
Où une étoile descendra sur tes bagages de sable

I'll enter yours to sound the depth of your tears
My appeals will leave you a little uncertain
And in the train made of glass turtles
You won't have to pull the emergency cord
You'll arrive alone on that lost shore
Where a star will alight on your luggage of sand

NON-LIEU

Art des jours art des nuits
La balance des blessures qui s'appelle Pardonne
Balance rouge et sensible au poids d'un vol d'oiseau
Quand les écuyères au col de neige les mains vides
Poussent leurs chars de vapeur sur les prés
Cette balance sans cesse affolée je la vois
Je vois l'ibis aux belles manières
Qui revient de l'étang lacé dans mon cœur
Les roues du rêve charment les splendides ornières
Qui se lèvent très haut sur les coquilles de leurs robes
Et l'étonnement bondit de-ci de-là sur la mer
Partez ma chère aurore n'oubliez rien de ma vie
Prenez ces roses qui grimpent au puits des miroirs
Prenez les battements de tous les cils
Prenez jusqu'aux fils qui soutiennent les pas des
    danseurs de corde et des gouttes d'eau
Art des jours art des nuits
Je suis à la fenêtre très loin dans une cité pleine
    d'épouvante
Dehors des hommes à chapeau claque se suivent à
    intervalle régulier
Pareils aux pluies que j'aimais
Alors qu'il faisait si beau
« A la rage de Dieu » est le nom d'un cabaret où je suis
    entré hier

NO INDICTMENT

Art of days art of nights
The scale of wounds called Forgive
Red scale sensitive to the weight of a bird's flight
When empty-handed women on horseback with snowy collars
Drive their chariots of mist over the meadows
That scale continually driven mad I see it
I see the ibis with its lovely manners
Returning from the pool laced into my heart
The wheels of the dream charm the splendid ruts
Which raise themselves very high on the shells of their dresses
And astonishment bounds here and there on the sea
Go my dear sunrise forget nothing of my life
Take these roses that climb the wells of mirrors
Take the flutter of all eyelashes
Take even the wires that hold up the steps of the tightrope walkers and drops of water
Art of days art of nights
I'm at the window far away in a city filled with terror
Men outside in top hats go by at regular intervals
Like the rains I loved
Even though the weather was so beautiful
"The Wrath of God" is the name of a cabaret I went into yesterday

Il est écrit sur la devanture blanche en lettres plus
    pâles
Mais les femmes-marins qui glissent derrière les vitres
Sont trop heureuses pour être peureuses
Ici jamais de corps toujours l'assassinat sans preuves
Jamais le ciel toujours le silence
Jamais la liberté que pour la liberté

It's written on the white front in letters even more pale
But the sailor girls who glide behind the windowpanes
Scarcely have cares so they never have scares
Here never a body always the murder with no clues
Never sky always silence
Never freedom except for freedom

SUR LA ROUTE QUI MONTE ET DESCEND

Dites-moi où s'arrêtera la flamme
Existe-t-il un signalement des flammes
Celle-ci corne à peine le papier
Elle se cache dans les fleurs et rien ne l'alimente
Mais on voit dans les yeux et l'on ne sait pas non plus ce qu'on voit dans les yeux
Puisqu'ils vous voient
Une statue est agenouillée sur la mer mais
Ce n'est plus la mer
Les phares se dressent maintenant dans la ville
Ils barrent la route aux blocs merveilleux de glace et de chair
Qui précipitaient dans l'arène leurs innombrables chars
La poussière endort les femmes en habits de reines
Et la flamme court toujours
C'est une fraise de dentelle au cou d'un jeune seigneur
C'est l'imperceptible sonnerie d'une cloche de paille dans la maison d'un poète ou de quelque autre vaurien
C'est l'hémisphère boréal tout entier
Avec ses lampes suspendues ses pendules qui se posent
C'est ce qui monte du précipice à l'heure du rendez-vous
Les cœurs sont les rames légères de cet océan perdu
Lorsque les signaux tournent au bord des voies avec un bruit sec

ON THE ROAD THAT GOES UP AND DOWN

Tell me where the flame will stop
Are there vital statistics for flames
This one barely dog-ears the paper
It hides in flowers and nothing feeds it
But we look in its eyes and don't know what we see in its
  eyes any more
Because they are looking at you
A statue is kneeling on the sea but
It isn't the sea any more
Now lighthouses rise up in the city
They bar the way to marvelous blocks of ice and flesh
That were plunging their countless chariots into the arena
The dust puts to sleep women dressed as queens
And the flame keeps on running
It's a lace ruff around the neck of a young lord
It's the imperceptible chiming of a straw clock in the house
  of a poet or some other good-for-nothing
It's the whole boreal hemisphere
With its hanging lamps its pendulums coming in for a
  landing
It's what climbs the cliff at the appointed hour
Hearts are the light oars of that lost ocean
While roadside stoplights change with a dry click

Qui ressemble à ce craquement spécial sous les pas des prêtres
Il n'y a plus d'actrice en tournée dans les wagons blanc et or
Qui la tête à la portière justement des pensées d'eau très grandes couvrent les mares
Ne s'attende à ce que la flamme lui confère l'oubli définitif de son rôle
Les étiquettes effacées des bouteilles vertes parlent encore de châteaux
Mais ces châteaux sont déserts à l'exception d'une chevelure vivante
Château-Ausone
Et cette chevelure qui ne s'attarde point à se défaire
Flotte sur l'air méduse C'est la flamme
Elle tourne maintenant autour d'une croix
Méfiez-vous elle profanerait votre tombe
Sous terre la méduse est encore chez elle
Et la flamme aux ailes de colombe n'escorte que les voyageurs en danger
Elle fausse compagnie aux amants dès qu'ils sont deux à être seuls
Où va-t-elle je vois se briser les glaces de Venise aux approches de Venise
Je vois s'ouvrir des fenêtres détachées de toute espèce de mur sur un chantier
Là des ouvriers nus font le bronze plus clair

Like that special crunching made by priests when they
walk
There's no actress on tour any more in the white and gold
wagon
Who with her head just poking out of the door-curtain
her great water-thoughts covering the pond
Expects only that the flame will grant her the ultimate
oblivion of her role
The worn labels of green bottles still speak of chateaus
But the chateaus are deserted except for a living head of
hair
Chateau-Ausone
And the hair that never stays up late to comb itself out
Floats on the air the medusa jellyfish It's the flame
Now it circles around a cross
Beware lest it desecrate your grave
Beneath the earth the medusa jellyfish is still at home
And the flame with dove's wings accompanies only trav-
elers in danger
It gives the slip to lovers the moment the two of them are
alone
Where is it going I see the mirrors of Venice smashing on
the outskirts of Venicc
I see windows that aren't attached to any kind of wall
opening at a construction site
Some naked workers there polish the bronze brighter

Ce sont des tyrans trop doux pour que contre eux se
soulèvent les pierres
Ils ont des bracelets aux pieds qui sont faits de ces pierres
Les parfums gravitent autour d'eux étoile de la myrrhe
terre du foin
Ils connaissent les pays pluvieux dévoilés par les perles
Un collier de perles fait un moment paraître grise la
flamme
Mais aussitôt une couronne de flammes s'incorpore les
perles immortelles
A la naissance d'un bois qui doit sauver de la destruction
les seules essences des plantes
Prennent part un homme et tout en haut d'une rampe
d'escalier de fougère
Plusieurs femmes groupées sur les dernières marches
Elles ouvrent et ferment les yeux comme les poupées
L'homme que je ne suis plus cravache alors la dernière
bête blanche
Qui s'évanouit dans la brume du matin
Sa volonté sera-t-elle faite
Dans le premier berceau de feuillage la flamme tombe
comme un hochet
Sous ses yeux on jette le filet des racines
Un couvert d'argent sur une toile d'araignée
Mais la flamme elle ne saurait reprendre haleine
Malheur à une flamme qui reprendrait haleine
Je pense à une flamme barbare

These tyrants are too gentle for stones to rise up against
them
They wear rings on their feet made from these stones
Perfumes hover around them star of myrrh field of hay
They know the rainy lands unveiled by pearls
A pearl necklace makes the flame seem grey for a moment
But immediately a crown of flames encompasses the
immortal pearls
A man and at the head of a fern stairway
Several women grouped on the top steps
Who open and close their eyes like dolls
Assist at the birth of a forest that must save
The very essences of plants from destruction
The man I no longer am then horsewhips the last white
beast
Which vanishes in the morning mist
Shall its will be done
In the first cradle of foliage the flame falls like a baby's
rattle
Beneath its eyes they toss the net of roots
A silver place-setting on a spider web
But the flame won't know how to catch its breath again
Woe betide the flame that would catch its breath
I think of a barbaric flame

Comme celle qui passant dans ce restaurant de nuit
brûle aux doigts des femmes les éventails
Comme celle qui marche à toute heure sur ma trace
Et luit à la tombée des feuilles dans chaque feuille qui
tombe
Flamme d'eau guide-moi jusqu'à la mer de feu

Like the one that burns the fans in women's fingers as it
    passes through this all-night restaurant
Like the one that trails me night and day
And gleams in each falling leaf when the leaves fall
Flame of water guide me to the sea of fire

LES ATTITUDES SPECTRALES

Je n'attache aucune importance à la vie
Je n'épingle pas le moindre papillon de vie à l'importance
Je n'importe pas à la vie
Mais les rameaux du sel les rameaux blancs
Toutes les bulles d'ombre
Et les anémones de mer
Descendent et respirent à l'intérieur de ma pensée
Ils viennent des pleurs que je ne verse pas
Des pas que je ne fais pas qui sont deux fois des pas
Et dont le sable se souvient à la marée montante
Les barreaux sont à l'intérieur de la cage
Et les oiseaux viennent de très haut chanter devant ces barreaux
Un passage souterrain unit tous les parfums
Un jour une femme s'y engagea
Cette femme devint si brillante que je ne pus la voir
De ces yeux qui m'ont vu moi-même brûler
J'avais déjà cet âge que j'ai
Et je veillais sur moi sur ma pensée comme un gardien de nuit dans une immense fabrique
Seul gardien
Le rond-point enchantait toujours les mêmes tramways
Les figures de plâtre n'avaient rien perdu de leur expression
Elles mordaient la figue du sourire
Je connais une draperie dans une ville disparue

GHOSTLY STANCES

I don't attach any importance to life
I don't pin life's least butterfly to importance
I'm unimportant to life
But branches of salt white branches
All the bubbles of shadow
And sea anemones
Dive down and breathe deep inside my thought
They come from tears I don't shed
From steps I don't take that are steps twice over
And that sand remembers when the tide rises
The bars are inside the cage
And birds come from high up to sing in front of these bars
An underground passage connects all perfumes
One day a woman entered it
That woman grew so radiant I couldn't see her
With these eyes that have even seen me burning
I was already as old as I am now
And I watched over myself over my thoughts like a night
    watchman in an immense factory
The only watchman
The traffic circle still cast its spell over the same trolleys
The expressions on the plaster figurines hadn't changed
They were chewing the smile's rye
I know of a cloth in a vanished city

S'il me plaisait de vous apparaître vêtu de cette draperie
Vous croiriez à l'approche de votre fin
Comme à la mienne
Enfin les fontaines comprendraient qu'il ne faut pas dire Fontaine
On attire les loups avec les miroirs de neige
Je possède une barque détachée de tous les climats
Je suis entraîné par une banquise aux dents de flamme
Je coupe et je fends le bois de cet arbre qui sera toujours vert
Un musicien se prend dans les cordes de son instrument
Le Pavillon Noir du temps d'aucune histoire d'enfance
Aborde un vaisseau qui n'est encore que le fantôme du sien
Il y a peut-être une garde à cette épée
Mais dans cette garde il y a déjà un duel
Au cours duquel les deux adversaires se désarment
Le mort est le moins offensé
L'avenir n'est jamais

Les rideaux qui n'ont jamais été levés
Flottent aux fenêtres des maisons qu'on construira
Les lits faits de tous les lys
Glissent sous les lampes de rosée
Un soir viendra
Les pépites de lumière s'immobilisent sous la mousse bleue

If I felt like appearing before you draped in that cloth
You'd think your end was drawing near
Just like mine
Fountains would finally understand that they shouldn't say Fountain
Wolves are lured with snow mirrors
I own a boat that isn't moored to any climate
I'm swept along by an ice floe with flaming teeth
I chop and split the wood of the tree that will always be green
A musician gets caught in the strings of his instrument
The Jolly Roger from the time of any children's story
Boards a vessel that is only the ghost of itself
Maybe there's a hilt on that sword
But in that hilt there's already a duel
During which the two opponents disarm each other
The dead one is the less-offended party
It's never the future

Curtains that have never been opened
Float in the windows of houses yet to be built
Beds made of all lily beds
Slide under lamps of dew
An evening will come
Nuggets of light roll to a stop under blue moss

Les mains qui font et défont les nœuds de l'amour et de l'air
Gardent toute leur transparence pour ceux qui voient
Ils voient les palmes sur les mains
Les couronnes dans les yeux
Mais le brasier des couronnes et des palmes
S'allume ne fait à peine que s'allumer au plus profond de la forêt
Là où les cerfs mirent en penchant la tête les années
On n'entend encore qu'un faible battement
D'où procèdent mille bruits plus légers ou plus sourds
Et ce battement se perpétue
Il y a des robes qui vibrent
Et leur vibration est à l'unisson de ce battement
Mais quand je veux voir le visage de celles qui les portent
Un grand brouillard se lève de terre
Au bas des clochers derrière les plus élégants réservoirs de vie et de richesse
Dans les gorges qui s'obscurcissent entre deux montagnes
Sur la mer à l'heure où le soleil fraîchit
Les êtres qui me font signe sont séparés par des étoiles
Et pourtant la voiture lancée au grand galop
Emporte jusqu'à ma dernière hésitation
Qui m'attend là-bas dans la ville où les statues de bronze et de pierre ont changé de place avec les statues de cire
Banians banians

The hands that tie and untie love-knots and air-knots
Keep all their transparency for those who see
They see palms on hands
Crowns in eyes
But the brazier of crowns and palms
Catches fire just barely catches fire at the deepest part of the forest
There where stags lower their heads to take aim at the years
Now all you can hear is a dull thud
From which come a thousand noises more faint or muffled
And this thud goes on
There are dresses that quiver
Quivering to the beat of this thud
But when I want to see the faces of the women who wear them
A huge fog rises from the ground
At the foot of steeples behind the most elegant reservoirs of life and wealth
In gorges that grow dark between two mountains
On the sea at the hour when the sun cools down
The beings who signal to me are separated by stars
And yet the carriage travelling at a gallop
Carries away my very last hesitation
Which waits for me over there in the city where the statues of bronze and stone have changed places with the wax statues
Banyans banyans

HOTEL DES ÉTINCELLES

Le papillon philosophique
Se pose sur l'étoile rose
Et cela fait une fenêtre de l'enfer
L'homme masqué est toujours debout devant la femme nue
Dont les cheveux glissent comme au matin la lumière sur un réverbère qu'on a oublié d'éteindre
Les meubles savants entraînent la pièce qui jongle
Avec ses rosaces
Ses rayons de soleil circulaires
Ses moulages de verre
A l'intérieur desquels bleuit un ciel au compas
En souvenir de la poitrine inimitable
Maintenant le nuage d'un jardin passe par-dessus la tête de l'homme qui vient de s'asseoir
Il coupe en deux la femme au buste de magie aux yeux de Parme
C'est l'heure où l'ours boréal au grand air d'intelligence
S'étire et compte un jour
De l'autre côté la pluie se cabre sur les boulevards d'une grande ville
La pluie dans le brouillard avec des traînées de soleil sur des fleurs rouges
La pluie et le diabolo des temps anciens
Les jambes sous le nuage fruitier font le tour de la serre

SPARKS HOTEL

The philosophical butterfly
Lands on the pink star
And that makes one of hell's windows
The man in the mask always stands in front of the naked woman
Whose hair glides like the light of a streetlamp they forgot to put out in the morning
The wise furniture drags along the room that juggles
Its rose windows
Its circular sunbeams
Its glass moldings
Deep inside them a compass sky turns blue
In memory of the inimitable breasts
Now the garden's cloud passes over the head of the man who's just sat down
It cuts in two the woman with the magic bust and the Parma eyes
It's the hour when the polar bear with such an intelligent face
Stretches and tallies another day
Across the street the rain rears up on the boulevards of a big city
The rain in the fog with traces of sun on red flowers
The rain and the diabolo of times gone by
The legs beneath the fruit-bearing cloud travel all around the greenhouse

On n'aperçoit plus qu'une main très blanche le pouls
est figuré par deux minuscules ailes
Le balancier de l'absence oscille entre les quatre murs
Fendant les têtes
D'où s'échappent des bandes de rois qui se font aussitôt
la guerre
Jusqu'à ce que l'éclipse orientale
Turquoise au fond des tasses
Découvre le lit équilatéral aux draps couleur de ces
fleurs dites boules-de-neige
Les guéridons charmants les rideaux lacérés
A portée d'un petit livre griffé de ces mots *Point
de lendemain*
Dont l'auteur porte un nom bizarre
Dans l'obscure signalisation terrestre

All we see is a very white hand its pulse represented by
    two minuscule wings
The pendulum of absence swings between four walls
Splitting in two the heads
From which bands of kings escape and immediately
    wage war on each other
Until the oriental eclipse
Turquoise at the bottom of cups
Reveals the equilateral bed with sheets the color of those
    flowers called snowballs
Charming night tables curtains torn to shreds
Within reach of a little book stamped with these words
    No Tomorrow
Whose author has a weird name
In the obscure signals of this world

LE VERBE ÊTRE

Je connais le désespoir dans ses grandes lignes. Le désespoir n'a pas d'ailes, il ne se tient pas nécessairement à une table desservie sur une terrasse, le soir, au bord de la mer. C'est le désespoir et ce n'est pas le retour d'une quantité de petits faits comme des graines qui quittent à la nuit tombante un sillon pour un autre. Ce n'est pas la mousse sur une pierre ou le verre à boire. C'est un bateau criblé de neige, si vous voulez, comme les oiseaux qui tombent et leur sang n'a pas la moindre épaisseur. Je connais le désespoir dans ses grandes lignes. Une forme très petite, délimitée par des bijoux de cheveux. C'est le désespoir. Un collier de perles pour lequel on ne saurait trouver de fermoir et dont l'existence ne tient pas même à un fil, voilà le désespoir. Le reste nous n'en parlons pas. Nous n'avons pas fini de désespérer si nous commençons. Moi je désespère de l'abat-jour vers quatre heures, je désespère de l'éventail vers minuit, je désespère de la cigarette des condamnés. Je connais le désespoir dans ses grandes lignes. Le désespoir n'a pas de cœur, la main reste toujours au désespoir hors d'haleine, au désespoir dont les glaces ne nous disent jamais s'il est mort. Je vis de ce désespoir qui m'enchante. J'aime cette mouche bleue qui vole dans le ciel à l'heure où les étoiles chantonnent. Je connais dans ses grandes lignes le désespoir aux longs étonnements grêles, le désespoir de la fierté, le désespoir de la colère. Je me lève chaque jour comme tout le monde et je détends les bras sur un papier à fleurs, je ne me souviens de rien et c'est toujours avec désespoir que je découvre les beaux arbres déracinés de la nuit. L'air de la chambre est beau comme des baguettes de tambour. Il fait un temps de temps. Je connais le désespoir dans ses grandes lignes. C'est comme le vent du rideau

THE VERB TO BE

I know the general outline of despair. Despair has no wings, it doesn't necessarily sit at a cleared table in the evening on a terrace by the sea. It's despair and not the return of a quantity of insignificant facts like seeds that leave one furrow for another at nightfall. It's not the moss that forms on a rock or the foam that rocks in a glass. It's a boat riddled with snow, if you will, like birds that fall and their blood doesn't have the slightest thickness. I know the general outline of despair. A very small shape, defined by jewels worn in the hair. That's despair. A pearl necklace for which no clasp can be found and whose existence can't even hang by a thread. That's despair for you. Let's not go into the rest. Once we begin to despair we don't stop. I myself despair of the lampshade around four o'clock, I despair of the fan towards midnight, I despair of the cigarette smoked by men on death row. I know the general outline of despair. Despair has no heart, my hand always touches breathless despair, the despair whose mirrors never tell us if it's dead. I live on the despair that enchants me. I love that blue fly hovering in the sky at the hour when the stars hum. I know the general outline of the despair with long slender surprises, the despair of pride, the despair of anger. I get up every day like everyone else and I stretch my arms against a floral wallpaper, I don't remember anything and it's always in despair that I discover the beautiful uprooted trees of night. The air in the room is as beautiful as drumsticks. What weathery weather. I know the general outline of despair. It's like the curtain's wind that holds out a helping hand. Can you imagine such a despair? Fire! Ah they're on their way.... Help! Here they come falling down the stairs.... And the ads in the newspa-

qui me tend la perche. A-t-on idée d'un désespoir pareil! Au feu! Ah ils vont encore venir... Au secours ! Les voici qui tombent dans l'escalier... Et les annonces de journal, et les réclames lumineuses le long du canal. Tas de sable, va, espèce de tas de sable! Dans ses grandes lignes le désespoir n'a pas d'importance. C'est une corvée d'arbres qui va encore faire une forêt, c'est une corvée d'étoiles qui va encore faire un jour de moins, c'est une corvée de jours de moins qui va encore faire ma vie.

per, and the illuminated signs along the canal. Sandpile, beat it, you dirty sandpile! In its general outline despair has no importance. It's a squad of trees that will eventually make a forest, it's a squad of stars that will eventually make one less day, it's a squad of one-less-days that will eventually make up my life.

LES ÉCRITS S'EN VONT

Le satin des pages qu'on tourne dans les livres moule une femme si belle
Que lorsqu'on ne lit pas on contemple cette femme avec tristesse
Sans oser lui parler sans oser lui dire qu'elle est si belle
Que ce qu'on va savoir n'a pas de prix
Cette femme passe imperceptiblement dans un bruit de fleurs
Parfois elle se retourne dans les saisons imprimées
Et demande l'heure ou bien encore elle fait mine de regarder des bijoux bien en face
Comme les créatures réelles ne font pas
Et le monde se meurt une rupture se produit dans les anneaux d'air
Un accroc à l'endroit du cœur
Les journaux du matin apportent des chanteuses dont la voix a la couleur du sable sur des rivages tendres et dangereux
Et parfois ceux du soir livrent passage à de toutes jeunes filles qui mènent des bêtes enchaînées
Mais le plus beau c'est dans l'intervalle de certaines lettres
Où des mains plus blanches que la corne des étoiles à midi
Ravagent un nid d'hirondelles blanches
Pour qu'il pleuve toujours

THE WRITINGS DEPART

The satin of pages we turn in books bodies forth a woman
 so beautiful
That when we aren't reading we contemplate this woman
 sadly
Without daring to speak to her without daring to tell her
 that she's so beautiful
That what we're going to find out is priceless
This woman passes imperceptibly in a rustling of flowers
Sometimes she turns around in the printed seasons
And asks the time or even pretends to look jewels straight
 in the eye
The way real creatures don't
And the world dies a break appears in the rings of the air
A rip in the surface of the heart
The morning papers bring women singers whose voices
 are the color of sand on soft dangerous shores
And sometimes the afternoon papers make way for very
 young girls leading animals on chains
But most beautiful of all is the space between certain
 letters
Where hands whiter than dog-eared stars at noon
Ravage a nest of white swallows
To make it rain forever

Si bas si bas que les ailes ne s'en peuvent plus mêler
Des mains d'où l'on remonte à des bras si légers que la vapeur des prés dans ses gracieux entrelacs au-dessus des étangs est leur imparfait miroir
Des bras qui ne s'articulent à rien d'autre qu'au danger exceptionnel d'un corps fait pour l'amour
Dont le ventre appelle les soupirs détachés des buissons pleins de voiles
Et qui n'a de terrestre que l'immense vérité glacée des traîneaux de regards sur l'étendue toute blanche
De ce que je ne reverrai plus
A cause d'un bandeau merveilleux
Qui est le mien dans le colin-maillard des blessures

So low so low that their wings can't mingle with it
anymore
Hands that lead us to arms so delicate that the meadow
mist in its graceful interlacing above the pools is their
imperfect mirror
Arms joined to none other than the amazing danger of a
body made for love
Whose belly summons detached sighs of bushes full of
veils
And that has nothing earthy about it but the immense icy
truth of the sleighs of glances on the totally white
expanse
Of what I'll never see again
Because of a marvelous bandage
My own in the blindman's bluff of wounds

LA FORÊT DANS LA HACHE

On vient de mourir mais je suis vivant et cependant je n'ai plus d'âme. Je n'ai plus qu'un corps transparent à l'intérieur duquel des colombes transparentes se jettent sur un poignard transparent tenu par une main transparente. Je vois l'effort dans toute sa beauté, l'effort réel qui ne se chiffre par rien, peu avant l'apparition de la dernière étoile. Le corps que j'habite comme une hutte et à forfait déteste l'âme que j'avais et qui surnage au loin. C'est l'heure d'en finir avec cette fameuse dualité qu'on m'a tant reprochée. Fini le temps où des yeux sans lumière et sans bagues puisaient le trouble dans les mares de la couleur. Il n'y a plus ni rouge ni bleu. Le rouge-bleu unanime s'efface à son tour comme un rouge-gorge dans les haies de l'inattention. On vient de mourir, — ni toi ni moi ni eux exactement mais nous tous, sauf moi qui survis de plusieurs façons ; j'ai encore froid, par exemple. En voilà assez. Du feu! Du feu! Ou bien des pierres pour que je les fende, ou bien des oiseaux pour que je les suive, ou bien des corsets pour que je les serre autour de la taille des femmes mortes, et qu'elles ressuscitent, et qu'elles m'aiment, avec leurs cheveux fatigants, leurs regards défaits! Du feu, pour qu'on ne soit pas mort pour des prunes à l'eau-de-vie, du feu pour que le chapeau de paille d'Italie ne soit pas seulement une pièce de théâtre! Allo, le gazon! Allo, la pluie! C'est moi l'irréel souffle de ce jardin. La couronne noire posée sur ma tête est un cri de corbeaux migrateurs car il n'y avait jusqu'ici que des enterrés vivants, d'ailleurs en petit nombre, et voici que je suis le premier *aéré mort*. Mais j'ai un corps pour ne plus m'en défaire, pour forcer les reptiles à m'admirer. Des mains sanglantes, des yeux de gui, une bouche de feuille morte et de verre (les feuilles mortes bougent sous

THE FOREST IN THE AXE

Someone just died but I'm still alive and yet I don't have a soul any more. All I have left is a transparent body inside of which transparent doves hurl themselves on a transparent dagger held by a transparent hand. I see struggle in all its beauty, real struggle that nothing can measure, just before the last star comes out. The rented body I live in like a hut detests the soul I had that floats in the distance. It's time to put an end to that famous dualism for which I've been so much reproached. Gone are the days when eyes without light and rings drew sediment from the pools of color. There's neither red nor blue any more. Unanimous red-blue fades away in turn like a robin redbreast in the hedges of inattention. Someone just died,—not you or I or they exactly, but all of us, except me who survives by a variety of means: I'm still cold for example. That's enough. A match! A match! Or how about some rocks so I can split them, or some birds so I can follow them, or some corsets so I can tighten them around dead women's waists, so they'll come back to life and love me, with their exhausting hair, their disheveled glances! A match, so no one dies for brandied plums, a match so the Italian straw hat can be more than a play! Hey, lawn! Hey, rain! *I'm* the unreal breath of this garden. The black crown resting on my head is a cry of migrating crows because up till now there have only been those who were buried alive, and only a few of them, and here I am the first *aerated dead man.* But I have a body so I can stop doing myself in, so I can force reptiles to admire me. Bloody hands, mistletoe eyes, a mouth of dried leaves and glass (the dried leaves move under the glass; they're not as red as one would think, when indifference exposes its voracious methods), hands

le verre; elles ne sont pas aussi rouges qu'on le pense, quand l'indifférence expose ses méthodes voraces), des mains pour te cueillir, thym minuscule de mes rêves, romarin de mon extrême pâleur. Je n'ai plus d'ombre non plus. Ah mon ombre, ma chère ombre. Il faut que j'écrive une longue lettre à cette ombre que j'ai perdue. Je commencerai par Ma chère ombre. Ombre, ma chérie. Tu vois. Il n'y a plus de soleil. Il n'y a plus qu'un tropique sur deux. Il n'y a plus qu'un homme sur mille. Il n'y a plus qu'une femme sur l'absence de pensée qui caractérise en noir pur cette époque maudite. Cette femme tient un bouquet d'immortelles de la forme de mon sang.

to gather you, miniscule thyme of my dreams, rosemary of my extreme pallor. I don't have a shadow any more, either. Ah my shadow, my dear shadow. I should write a long letter to the shadow I lost. I'd begin it My Dear Shadow. Shadow, my darling. You see. There's no more sun. There's only one tropic left out of two. There's only one man left in a thousand. There's only one woman left in the absence of thought that characterizes in pure black this cursed era. That woman holds a bouquet of everlastings shaped like my blood.

TOUTES LES ÉCOLIÈRES ENSEMBLE

Souvent tu dis marquant la terre du talon comme éclôt dans un buisson l'églantine
Sauvage qui n'a l'air faite que de rosée
Tu dis Toute la mer et tout le ciel pour une seule
Victoire d'enfance dans le pays de la danse ou mieux pour une seule
Étreinte dans le couloir d'un train
Qui va au diable avec les coups de fusil sur un pont ou mieux
Encore pour une seule farouche parole
Telle qu'en doit dire en vous regardant
Un homme sanglant dont le nom va très loin d'arbre en arbre
Qui ne fait qu'entrer et sortir parmi cent oiseaux de neige
Où donc est-ce bien
Et quand tu dis cela toute la mer et tout le ciel
S'éparpillent comme une nuée de petites filles dans la cour d'un pensionnat sévère
Après une dictée où *Le cœur m'en dit*
S'écrivait peut-être *Le cœur mendie*

ALL THE SCHOOLGIRLS TOGETHER

Sometimes you say marking the earth with your heel the
way in a bush the eglantine grows
Wild as if it's made only of dew
You say The whole sea and the whole sky for a single
Childhood victory in the land of dance or better for a
single
Embrace in the corridor of a train
Going to hell with gunshots on a bridge or better
Still for one savage word
The kind that a bleeding man whose name travels very
far
From tree to tree would say as he looked at you
All he does is go in and out in the middle of a hundred
snowbirds
Then where is this really
And when you say it the whole sea and the whole sky
Scatter like a thundercloud of girls in the playground of
a strict boarding school
After a dictation exercise in which *My heart bleeds*
Might have been written *My heart pleads*

NŒUD DES MIROIRS

Les belles fenêtres ouvertes et fermées
Suspendues aux lèvres du jour
Les belles fenêtres en chemise
Les belles fenêtres aux cheveux de feu dans la nuit noire
Les belles fenêtres de cris d'alarme et de baisers
Au-dessus de moi au-dessous de moi derrière moi il y en
    a moins qu'en moi
Où elles ne font qu'un seul cristal bleu comme les blés
Un diamant divisible en autant de diamants qu'il en
    faudrait pour se baigner à tous les bengalis
Et les saisons qui ne sont pas quatre mais quinze ou seize
En moi parmi lesquelles celle où le métal fleurit
Celle dont le sourire est moins qu'une dentelle
Celle où la rosée du soir unit les femmes et les pierres
Les saisons lumineuses comme l'intérieur d'une
    pomme dont on a détaché un quartier
Ou encore comme un quartier excentrique habité par
    des êtres qui sont de mèche avec le vent
Ou encore comme le vent de l'esprit qui la nuit ferre
    d'oiseaux sans bornes les chevaux à naseaux
    d'algèbre

KNOT OF MIRRORS

Open and closed the beautiful windows
Hung from the day's lips
The beautiful windows wearing only their nighties
The beautiful windows with hair of fire in the dark night
The beautiful windows of kisses and cries for help
Above me below me behind me there are fewer than inside me
Where all they add up to is a single crystal as blue as wheat
A diamond divisible into as many diamonds as you'd need to bathe every Bengali
And the seasons which aren't four but fifteen or sixteen
Inside me among them the one where metal blossoms
The one whose smile is less than a piece of lace
The one where evening's dew unites women and rocks
The seasons luminous as the inside of an apple with one section removed
Or like a section of the suburbs inhabited by beings in cahoots with the wind
Or like the mind's wind which at night puts shoes of endless birds on horses with algebra nostrils

Ou encore comme la formule

Teinture de passiflore Teinture d'aubépine	{ aa 50 cent. cubes
Teinture de gui	5 cent. cubes
Teinture de scille	3 cent, cubes

qui combat le bruit de galop

Les saisons remontent maille par maille leur filet brillant de l'eau vive de mes yeux
Et dans cc filet il y a ce que j'ai vu c'est la spire d'un fabuleux coquillage
Qui me rappelle l'exécution en vase clos de l'empereur Maximilien
Il y a ce que j'ai aimé c'est le plus haut rameau de l'arbre de corail qui sera foudroyé
C'est le style du cadran solaire à minuit vrai
Il y a ce que je connais bien ce que je connais si peu que prête-moi tes serres vieux délire
Pour m'élever avec mon cœur le long de la cataracte
Les aéronautes parlent de l'efflorescence de l'air en hiver

Or like the prescription

Tincture of passionflower	{	50 cubic cent. of ea.
Tincture of hawthorn		
Tincture of mistletoe		5 cubic cent.
Tincture of squills		3 cubic cent.
		that fights gallop rhythm

Link by link the seasons climb back up their net shining
with the spring water of my eyes
And in this net there's something I've seen it's the whorl
of a fabulous seashell
Which reminds me of the Emperor Maximilian's lonely
execution
There's something I've loved it's the highest bough of a
coral tree about to be struck by lightning
It's the sundial's *style* at exactly midnight
There's the things I really know and the things I know so
little about
so lend me your claws old delirium
And lift me with my heart along the cataract
Balloonists speak of the air's efflorescence in winter

UN HOMME ET UNE FEMME ABSOLUMENT BLANCS

Tout au fond de l'ombrelle je vois les prostituées merveilleuses
Leur robe un peu passée du côté du réverbère couleur des bois
Elles promènent avec elles un grand morceau de papier mural
Comme on ne peut en contempler sans serrement de cœur aux anciens étages d'une maison en démolition
Ou encore une coquille de marbre blanc tombée d'une cheminée
Ou encore un filet de ces chaînes qui derrière elles se brouillent dans les miroirs
Le grand instinct de la combustion s'empare des rues où elles se tiennent
Comme des fleurs grillées
Les yeux au loin soulevant un vent de pierre
Tandis qu'elles s'abîment immobiles au centre du tourbillon
Rien n'égale pour moi le sens de leur pensée inappliquée
La fraîcheur du ruisseau dans lequel leurs bottines trempent l'ombre de leur bec
La réalité de ces poignées de foin coupé dans lesquelles elle disparaissent
Je vois leur seins qui mettent une pointe de soleil dans la nuit profonde

A MAN AND A WOMAN COMPLETELY WHITE

Deep in the parasol I see the marvelous prostitutes
Next to the streetlamp the color of the forest their clothes
a little out of fashion
They carry around a big piece of wallpaper as they walk
The kind that always breaks your heart on the old walls
of a house being torn down
Or else a white marble seashell fallen from a mantel
Or else those strings of necklaces that get all tangled up
in the mirrors behind them
Their great instinct for combustion seizes the streets where
they stand
Like grilled flowers
Their eyes raising a wind of stone in the distance
While they are swallowed motionless at the center of the
whirlwind
For me nothing equals the meaning of their random
thoughts
The coolness of the stream where their little boots dip the
shadows of their beaks
The reality of those wisps of mown hay into which they
disappear
I see their breasts putting a dot of sun in deep night

Et dont le temps de s'abaisser et de s'élever est la seule mesure exacte de la vie
Je vois leurs seins qui sont des étoiles sur des vagues
Leurs seins dans lesquels pleure à jamais l'invisible lait bleu

And whose rise and fall is the only exact measurement of
life
I see their breasts that are stars on waves
Their breasts in which invisible blue milk weeps forever

FACTEUR CHEVAL

Nous les oiseaux que tu charmes toujours du haut de ces belvédères
Et qui chaque nuit ne faisons qu'une branche fleurie de tes épaules aux bras de ta brouette bien-aimée
Qui nous arrachons plus vifs que des étincelles à ton poignet
Nous sommes les soupirs de la statue de verre qui se soulève sur le coude quand l'homme dort
Et que des brèches brillantes s'ouvrent dans son lit
Brèches par lesquelles on peut apercevoir des cerfs aux bois de corail dans une clairière
Et des femmes nues tout au fond d'une mine
Tu t'en souviens tu te levais alors tu descendais du train
Sans un regard pour la locomotive en proie aux immenses racines barométriques
Qui se plaint dans la forêt vierge de toutes ses chaudières meurtries
Ses cheminées fumant de jacinthes et mue par des serpents bleus
Nous te précédions alors nous les plantes sujettes à métamorphoses
Qui chaque nuit nous faisons des signes que l'homme peut surprendre
Tandis que sa maison s'écroule et qu'il s'étonne devant les emboîtements singuliers

CHEVAL THE MAILMAN

We are the birds you always charm down from the top of these belvederes
Who every night become one blossoming branch from your shoulders to the arms of the wheelbarrow you love so much
We who tear ourselves away from your wrist livelier than sparks
We're the sighs of the glass statue that raises itself onto one elbow when mankind is sleeping
And may shining crevices open in his bed
Crevices through which you can see stags with coral antlers in a clearing
And naked women deep at the bottom of a mine
You remember you woke up then you stepped off the train
Without glancing at the locomotive preyed upon by immense barometric roots
Which complains in the virgin forest about all its battered boilers
Its smokestacks spewing hyacinths and driven by blue snakes
Then we preceded you we the plants subject to metamorphoses
Who every night send signals that man can accidentally detect
While his house falls to ruins and he stands amazed by the unique joints

Que recherche son lit avec le corridor et l'escalier
L'escalier se ramifie indéfiniment
Il mène à une porte de meule il s'élargit tout à coup sur une place publique
Il est fait de dos de cygnes une aile ouverte pour la rampe
Il tourne sur lui-même comme s'il allait se mordre
Mais non il se contente sur nos pas d'ouvrir toutes ses marches comme des tiroirs
Tiroirs de pain tiroirs de vin tiroirs de savon tiroirs de glaces tiroirs d'escaliers
Tiroirs de chair à la poignée de cheveux
A cette heure où des milliers de canards de Vaucanson se lissent les plumes
Sans te retourner tu saisissais la truelle dont on fait les seins
Nous te souriions tu nous tenais par la taille
Et nous prenions les attitudes de ton plaisir
Immobiles sous nos paupières pour toujours comme la femme aime voir l'homme
Après avoir fait l'amour

That his bed tries to form with the hallway and the staircase
The staircase branches out endlessly
It leads to a grindstone door it suddenly widens onto a public square
It's made out of swans' backs one wing open for the bannister
It turns around as if to bite itself
But no Following in our footsteps it's content to open all its steps like drawers
Bread drawers wine drawers soap drawers mirror drawers staircase drawers
Flesh drawers with hair handles
At the time of day when thousands of Vaucanson ducks preen their feathers
Without looking back you grabbed the trowel that breasts are made with
We smiled at you you had your arms around our waists
And we held the poses of your pleasure
Motionless under our eyelids forever the way a woman likes to see a man
After they've made love

RIDEAU RIDEAU

Les théâtres vagabonds des saisons qui auront joué ma vie
Sous mes sifflets
L'avant-scène avait été aménagée en cachot d'où je pouvais siffler
Les mains aux barreaux je voyais sur fond de verdure noire
L'héroïne nue jusqu'à la ceinture
Qui se suicidait au début du premier acte
La pièce se poursuivait inexplicablement dans le lustre
La scène se couvrant peu à peu de brouillard
Et je criais parfois
Je brisais la cruche qu'on m'avait donnée et de laquelle s'échappaient des papillons
Qui montaient follement vers le lustre
Sous prétexte d'intermède encore de ballet qu'on tenait à me donner de mes pensées
J'essayais alors de m'ouvrir le poignet avec les morceaux de terre brune
Mais c'étaient des pays dans lesquels je m'étais perdu
Impossible de retrouver le fil de ces voyages
J'étais séparé de tout par le pain du soleil
Un personnage circulait dans la salle seul personnage agile
Qui s'était fait un masque de mes traits

CURTAIN CURTAIN

The traveling theaters of the seasons that played my life
While I booed
The proscenium had been converted into a prison cell from which I could hiss
With my hands on the bars I saw a backdrop of dark green
The heroine naked to the waist
Who committed suicide at the beginning of the first act
Inexplicably the play continued in the chandelier
Little by little the stage filled with fog
And sometimes I cried out
I broke the pitcher they had given me from which butterflies escaped
And rose madly towards the chandelier
Under the pretext of another ballet interlude of my thoughts that they insisted on performing for me
I then tried to slash my wrist with bits of brown earth
But those were lands where I got lost
Impossible to pick up the thread of these travels
I was separated from everything by the bread of the sun
A character moved around the theater the only active character
Who had made himself a mask with my features

Il prenait odieusement parti pour l'ingénue et pour le traître
Le bruit courait que c'était arrangé comme mai juin juillet août
Soudain la caverne se faisait plus profonde
Dans les couloirs interminables des bouquets tenus à hauteur de main
Erraient seuls c'est à peine si j'osais entrouvrir ma porte
Trop de liberté m'était accordée à la fois
Liberté de m'enfuir en traîneau de mon lit
Liberté de faire revivre les êtres qui me manquent
Les chaises d'aluminium se resserraient autour d'un kiosque de glaces
Sur lequel se levait un rideau de rosée frangé de sang devenu vert
Liberté de chasser devant moi les apparences réelles
Le sous-sol était merveilleux sur un mur blanc apparaissait en pointillé de feu ma silhouette percée au cœur d'une balle

Hatefully he took the side of the ingénue and the traitor
The rumor was that it had been organized as easy as one two three
Suddenly the cave grew deeper
In the endless corridors bouquets held hand-high
Wandered alone I hardly dared to open my door a crack
All at once too much freedom had been given to me
The freedom to run away in a sleigh from my bed
The freedom to bring back to life the beings that I missed
Aluminum chairs were closing in around a kiosk of mirrors
Over which rose a curtain of dew fringed with blood that had turned green
The freedom to chase away the real apparitions before me
The basement was marvelous on a white wall my silhouette appeared in fiery dots pierced through the heart by a bullet

LE SPHINX VERTÉBRAL

La belle ombre patiente et courbe fait le tour des pavés
Les fenêtres vénitiennes s'ouvrent et se ferment sur la place
Où vont en liberté des bêtes suivies de feux
Les réverbères mouillés bruissent encadrés d'une nuée d'yeux bleus
Qui couvrent le paysage en amont de la ville
Ce matin proue du soleil comme tu t'engloutis dans les superbes chants exhalés à l'ancienne derrière les rideaux par les guetteuses nues
Tandis que les arums géants tournent autour de leur taille
Et que le mannequin sanglant saute sur ses trois pieds dans le grenier
Il vient disent-elles en cambrant leur cou sur lequel le bondissement des nattes libère des glaciers à peine roses
Qui se fendent sous le poids d'un rai de lumière tombant des persiennes arrachées
Il vient c'est le loup aux dents de verre
Celui qui mange l'heure dans les petites boîtes rondes
Celui qui souffle les parfums trop pénétrants des herbes
Celui qui fume les petits feux de passage le soir dans les navets
Les colonnes des grands appartements de marbre et de vétiver crient

THE VERTEBRAL SPHINX

Patient and curved the beautiful shadow takes a trip around the cobblestones
Venetian windows open and close on the square
Where beasts run free followed by traffic lights
Wet streetlamps hum framed by a blue-eyed storm cloud
That covers the countryside upriver from the city
This morning prow of the sun how you're engulfed by wonderful songs crooned in the old style by naked women watching behind curtains
While giant arums wind around their waists
And the bleeding mannequin hops on its three feet in the attic
He's coming say the women as they crane their necks where bouncing braids unleash slightly pink glaciers
That crack under the weight of a ray of light falling from torn-open shutters
He's coming the wolf with glass teeth
The one who eats time in little round boxes
The one who breathes the all-too-penetrating aromas of herbs
The one who gives the third degree all night in the turnip patch
The columns of marble and vetiver state chambers cry out

Elles crient elles sont prises de ces mouvements de
va-et-vient qui n'animaient jusque-là que certaines
pièces colossales des usines
Les femmes immobiles sur les plaques tournantes
vont voir
Il fait jour à gauche mais nuit complètement nuit à droite
Il y a des branchages encore pleins d'oiseaux qui passent
à toute allure obscurcissant le trou de la croisée
Des oiseaux blancs qui pondent des œufs noirs
Où sont ces oiseaux que remplacent maintenant des
étoiles bordées de deux rangs de perles
Une tête de poisson très très longue ce n'est pas encore
lui
De la tête de poisson naissent des jeunes filles secouant
un tamis
Et du tamis des cœurs faits de larmes bataviques
Il vient c'est le loup aux dents de verre
Celui qui volait très haut sur les terrains vagues reparus
au-dessus des maisons
Avec des plantes aiguisées toutes tournées vers ses yeux
D'un vert à défier une bouteille de mousse renversée
sur la neige
Ses griffes de jade dans lesquelles il se mire en volant
Son poil de la couleur des étincelles
C'est lui qui gronde dans les forges au crépuscule et
dans les lingeries abandonnées
Il est visible on le touche il avance avec son balancier
sur le fil tendu d'hirondelles

They cry out they're caught up in the motion of coming
and going which until then had driven only certain
colossal rooms in factories
Women motionless on turntables are going to take a look
It's daytime to the left but night completely night to the
right
There are branches still full of birds that pass by at full
speed blocking out the casement window opening
White birds that lay black eggs
Where are those birds now being replaced by stars
surrounded by two strings of pearls
A very very long fishhead that's not him yet
Young girls shaking a sieve are born from the fishhead
And hearts made of Prince Rupert's Drop are born from
the sieve
He's coming the wolf with glass teeth
The one who flew so high over the empty lots who
reappeared above the housetops
With sharp plants all turned toward his eyes
Green enough to challenge a bottle of foam spilled on the
snow
His jade claws in which he admires himself as he flies
His coat the color of sparks
He's the one snarling in the ironworks at dusk and in
abandoned linen closets
He's visible someone touches him he walks out with his
balancing pole on the tightrope made out of swallows

Les guetteuses se penchent se penchent aux fenêtres
De tout leur côté d'ombre de tout leur côté de lumière
La bobine du jour est tirée par petits coups du côté
du paradis de sable
Les pédales de la nuit bougent sans interruption

The women watching lean out lean out of their windows
With all of their darkness with all of their light
The day's bobbin is jerked a little at a time in the direction
  of the sand paradise
The pedals of the night keep on moving

VIGILANCE

A Paris la tour Saint-Jacques chancelante
Pareille à un tournesol
Du front vient quelquefois heurter la Seine et son ombre glisse imperceptiblement parmi les remorqueurs
A ce moment sur la pointe des pieds dans mon sommeil
Je me dirige vers la chambre où je suis étendu
Et j'y mets le feu
Pour que rien ne subsiste de ce consentement qu'on m'a arraché
Les meubles font alors place à des animaux de même taille qui me regardent fraternellement
Lions dans les crinières desquels achèvent de se consumer les chaises
Squales dont le ventre blanc s'incorpore le dernier frisson des draps
A l'heure de l'amour et des paupières bleues
Je me vois brûler à mon tour je vois cette cachette solennelle de riens
Qui fut mon corps
Fouillée par les becs patients des ibis du feu
Lorsque tout est fini j'entre invisible dans l'arche
Sans prendre garde aux passants de la vie qui font sonner très loin leurs pas traînants
Je vois les arêtes du soleil
A travers l'aubépine de la pluie

VIGILANCE

In Paris the Saint-Jacques Tower tottering
Like a sunflower
Sometimes bumps its forehead against the Seine and its shadow glides imperceptibly among the tugboats
At that moment on tiptoe in my sleep
I head for the room where I'm lying
And I set it on fire
So that nothing survives of the consent torn from me
Then the furniture makes room for animals of the same size that watch me like a brother
Lions in whose manes the chairs are finally burnt up
Dogfish whose white bellies blend with the last shiver of the bedsheets
At the hour of love and blue eyelids
Next I see myself burning I see that solemn hiding-place of nothings
That was my body
Raked by the patient beaks of the ibises of the fire
When it's all over invisible I board the ark
Without noticing life's pedestrians who make their shuffling steps echo far away
I see the fishbones of the sun
Through the hawthorn of the rain

J'entends se déchirer le linge humain comme une
grande feuille
Sous l'ongle de l'absence et de la présence qui sont de
connivence
Tous les métiers se fanent il ne reste d'eux qu'une
dentelle parfumée
Une coquille de dentelle qui a la forme parfaite d'un sein
Je ne touche plus que le cœur des choses je tiens le fil

I hear the human linen being torn like a great leaf
Beneath the fingernail of absence and presence which are
 in cahoots
All the looms fade nothing's left of them but a perfumed
 piece of lace
A seashell of lace in the perfect shape of a breast
All I touch is the heart of things I hold the thread

SANS CONNAISSANCE

On n'a pas oublié
La singulière tentative d'enlèvement
Tiens une étoile pourtant il fait encore grand jour
De cette jeune fille de quatorze ans
Quatre de plus que de doigts
Qui regagnait en ascenseur
Je vois ses seins comme si elle était nue
On dirait des mouchoirs séchant sur un rosier
L'appartement de ses parents
Le père un piquet solidement enfoncé dans l'ombre la mère jolie pyramide d'abat-jour
Appartement situé au quatrième étage d'un immeuble de la rue Saint-Martin
Non loin de la Porte gardée par deux salamandres géantes
Sous laquelle je me tiens moi-même plusieurs heures par jour
Que je sois à Paris ou non
La belle Euphorbe appelons la jeune fille Euphorbe
S'inquiète de l'arrêt de l'ascenseur entre le deuxième et le troisième étage
A six heures du soir quand le quartier Saint-Martin commence à broyer de la craie du plantain du vitrail
Rester ainsi suspendue comme une aiguillette à une veste mexicaine
N'a rien de particulièrement réjouissant

UNCONSCIOUS

Who could forget
The strange attempt to kidnap
Look a star though it's still broad daylight
That fourteen-year-old girl
Four more than fingers
Who was taking the elevator back to
I see her breasts as if she were naked
You'd say they were handkerchiefs drying on a rosebush
Her parents' apartment
Her father a stake solidly driven into his shadow her
  mother a pretty pyramid of a lampshade
An apartment located on the fifth floor of a building on
  the Rue Saint- Martin
Not far from the Gate of the same name guarded by two
  giant salamanders
I myself stand under it several hours a day
Whether I'm in Paris or not
Lovely Euphorbia let's call the girl Euphorbia
Is worried because the elevator has stopped between the
  third and fourth floors
At six o'clock in the evening when the Saint-Martin
  district begins to grind stained glass plantain chalk
Remaining suspended like a loop of gold braid on a
  Mexican vest
Isn't particularly entertaining

Le palier du second à quelques pieds au-dessous d'Euphorbe charrie des planches claires l'anguille d'une rampe et quelques jolies herbes noires très longues
Qui ressemblent à un vêtement d'homme
La jeune fille surprise en pleine ascension se compare à un diabolo de plumes
Elle a les yeux plus verts que d'ordinaire n'est verte l'angélique
Et ces yeux plongent se brûlent à d'autres yeux sur lesquels glisse une flamme de bore
D'en bas les mollets d'Euphorbe luisent un peu de biais ce sont deux oiseaux sombres qui doivent être plus tièdes et plus doux que tous les autres
Les yeux de bore s'y fixent un instant puis le regard étincelant s'évase dans la robe
Très fine qui est de Paris
C'en est assez pour que ces deux êtres se soient compris
Ainsi dans une hutte par temps de pluie sous les tropiques l'énervement fait merveille
Les insectes à taille minuscule déployant de véritables drapeaux qui traînent partout dans les coins
Une porte qui glisse sur elle-même avec le bruit d'une ombrelle qu'on ferme
L'enfant est dans les bras de l'homme il sent frémir la chair au-dessus des jarrets sous la robe qui remonte un peu comme un fuchsia

A few feet below Euphorbia the third floor landing carries along highly polished floor boards the eel of a staircase and some pretty and very tall black plants
Which look like a man's clothing
The young girl surprised on her way up compares herself to a feather diabolo
Her eyes are greener than the typical green of the angelica
And these eyes dive down burn themselves on other eyes that a boron flame glides across
Seen from below Euphorbia's calves gleam a little at an angle they are two somber birds that seem warmer and sweeter than all the others
The boron eyes stare at them for a moment then the flashing look escapes into her dress
Of fine quality and from Paris
That's all it takes for these two beings to understand each other
Thus in a hut during the rainy season in the tropics nervousness works miracles
Insects of minuscule size unfolding actual flags that lie around everywhere in the corners
A door that slides open with the sound of a closing umbrella
The child is in the man's arms he feels the flesh above her hams quiver under her dress hiked up a little like a fuchsia

L'escalier mal éclairé des ombres grandissent sur le mur de faux marbre chair
Ombres de chevaux lancés à toutes guides dans la tempête
Ombres de buissons qui courent à leur tour largement dépassés
Et surtout ombres de danseurs toujours le même couple sur une plaque tournante bordée de draps
Cet instant fait dérailler le train rond des pendules
La rue jette des éclairs Euphorbe sourit sournoisement entre la crainte et le plaisir
Je vois son cœur à cette minute il est distrait coupant il est le premier bourgeon qui saute d'un marronnier rose
Un mot et tout est sauvé
Un mot et tout est perdu
L'inconnu là la tentation comme nulle part ailleurs sous ce ciel à la paille de fer
Mais aussi la peur sous cette voûte affolante de pas qui vont et qui viennent
A faire un amas de plâtre de cette maison qui est bien loin
Un amas de plâtre dans un abri duquel on commencerait à s'aimer
La peur à oublier ses doigts dans un livre pour ne plus toucher
A fermer ses yeux dans le sillage du premier venu pour éperdument le fuir

The dimly-lit staircase the shadows lengthen on the wall
of imitation marble flesh
Shadows of horses dashing full rein into the storm
Shadows of sprinting hedges overtaken by many lengths
And above all shadows of dancers always the same couple
on a revolving platform hemmed with cloth
This instant derails the curved track of the pendulums
The street hurls thunderbolts Euphorbia slyly smiles somewhere between fear and pleasure
I see her heart at that moment it's distracted skipping a
beat it's the first bud to leap from a pink chestnut tree
One word and all is saved
One word and all is lost
There the unknown the temptation as nowhere else under
that iron filing sky
But also fear under that crazy vault of footsteps that come
and go
Turning that house so far away into a plaster heap
A plaster heap in a hideout where someone could begin
to love
Fear of forgetting her fingers in a book so as never to
touch again
Shutting her eyes in the wake of the first one so she can
desperately flee him

Quelle seconde
On sait le reste
Pfuût houch le coup de revolver le sang qui saute lestement les marches vertes
Pas assez vite pour que l'homme
Son signalement 1 m. 65 la concierge n'a pas osé arrêter ce visiteur inhabituel mais poli
Il était d'autre part très bien de sa personne
Ne s'éloigne en allumant une cigarette
Plus douce que la douleur d'aimer et d'être aime

What a moment
You know the rest
Bang ouch the gunshot the blood nimbly leaping the green stairs
Not quick enough to stop the man from
His description five feet four the concierge didn't dare stop this infrequent but polite visitor
He was moreover very good looking
Getting away as he lit a cigarette
Sweeter than the sadness of loving and being loved

DERNIÈRE LEVÉE

La lettre que j'attends voyage incognito dans une enveloppe
Que son timbre recouvre et au-delà
Ce timbre est oblitéré par le zodiaque
On a beaucoup de peine à déchiffrer mon nom dans sa dentelure
Quand elle me parviendra le soleil sera froid
Il y aura des épaves sur la place Blanche
Parmi lesquelles se distinguera mon courage
Pareil à un treuil d'écureuils
Je l'ouvrirai d'un coup de rame
Et je me mettrai à lire
Cela ne pourra manquer de provoquer un rassemblement
Mais je ne m'arrêterai pas
Les mots jamais entendus prendront le large
Ils seront de paille enflammée et luiront dans une cage d'amiante
Suspendue à l'arbre à devinettes
La lettre que j'attends sera de la couleur des voiliers éteints
Mais les nouvelles qu'elle m'apportera leurs formes de rosée
Je retrouverai dans ces formes tout ce que j'ai perdu
Ces lumières qui bercent les choses irréelles
Ces animaux dont les métamorphoses m'ont fait une raison

LAST MAIL PICKUP

The letter I'm waiting for travels incognito in an envelope
Covered by its stamp and beyond it
This stamp is obliterated by the zodiac
It's difficult to decipher my name in its perforations
When it reaches me the sun will be cold
There will be shipwrecks in the Place Blanche
Among which my courage will stand out
Like a winch of squirrels
I'll open it with one stroke of an oar
And I'll start reading
It can't miss drawing a crowd
But I won't stop
Words never heard before will set sail
They'll be made of blazing straw and will glow in an asbestos cage
Hung from a tree of riddles
The letter I'm waiting for will be the color of faded sailing ships
But the news it will bring me its dewy shapes
I'll find once more in those shapes everything I've lost
Those lights that cradle unreal things
Those animals whose metamorphoses have made me accept the inevitable

Ces pierres que je croyais lancées pour me dépister moi-même
Qu'elle est de petites dimensions cette lettre que j'attends
Pourvu qu'elle ne s'égare pas parmi les grains de poison

Those stones I thought were thrown to put me off my own
scent
How small are the dimensions of this letter I'm waiting for
I only hope it isn't lost among grains of poison

UNE BRANCHE D'ORTIE ENTRE PAR LA FENÊTRE

La femme au corps de papier peint
La tanche rouge des cheminées
Dont la mémoire est faite d'une multitude de petits abreuvoirs
Pour les navires au loin
Et qui rit comme un peu de braise qu'on aurait enchâssée dans la neige
Et qui se voit grandir et diminuer la nuit sur des pas d'accordéon
La cuirasse des herbes la poignée de la porte des poignards
Celle qui descend des paillettes du sphinx
Celle qui met des roulettes au fauteuil du Danube
Celle pour qui l'espace et le temps se déchirent le soir quand le veilleur de son œil vacille comme un elfe
N'est pas l'enjeu du combat que se livrent mes rêves
Oiseau cassant
Que la nature tend sur les fils télégraphiques des transes
Et qui chavire sur le grand lac de nombres de son chant
Elle est le double cœur de la muraille perdue
A laquelle s'agrippent les sauterelles du sang
Qui traînent mon apparence de miroir mes mains de faille
Mes yeux de chenilles mes cheveux de longues baleines noires
De baleines cachetées d'une cire étincelante et noire

A NETTLE BRANCH COMES IN THROUGH THE WINDOW

The woman with the wallpaper body
The red snapper of the fireplaces
Whose memory consists of a multitude of little watering holes
For boats in the distance
And who laughs like a glowing ember mounted in a setting of snow
And who sees herself grow larger and smaller at night on accordion steps
Cuirass of the grasses doorknob on the daggers' door
The woman who's descended from the spangles of the sphinx
The woman who puts casters on the Danube's armchair
The woman for whom space and time tear themselves up at night when the watchman in her eye twinkles like an elf
Isn't the prize of the fight that my dreams give in to
Brittle bird
That nature offers on the telegraph lines of fear
That capsizes on the huge lake of numbers of its song
She's the double heart of the lost wall
Gripped by the blood's grasshoppers
Pulling along my mirror image my hands lined with faults
My caterpillar eyes my hair of long black whales
Whales sealed with a glittering black wax

LE GRAND SECOURS MEURTRIER

La statue de Lautréamont
Au socle de cachets de quinine
En rase campagne
L'auteur des Poésies est couché à plat ventre
Et près de lui veille l'héloderme suspect
Son oreille gauche appliquée au sol est une boîte vitrée
Occupée par un éclair l'artiste n'a pas oublié de faire figurer au-dessus de lui
Le ballon bleu ciel en forme de tête de Turc
Le cygne de Montevideo dont les ailes sont déployées et toujours prêtes à battre
Lorsqu'il s'agit d'attirer de l'horizon les autres cygnes
Ouvre sur le faux univers deux yeux de couleurs différentes
L'un de sulfate de fer sur la treille des cils l'autre de boue diamantée
Il voit le grand hexagone à entonnoir dans lequel se crisperont bientôt les machines
Que l'homme s'acharne à couvrir de pansements
Il ravive de sa bougie de radium les fonds du creuset humain
Le sexe de plumes le cerveau de papier huilé
Il préside aux cérémonies deux fois nocturnes qui ont pour but soustraction faite du feu d'intervertir les cœurs de l'homme et de l'oiseau

THE DEADLY HELPING HAND

The statue of Lautréamont
Out on the plains
With its pedestal of quinine pills
The author of the Poems is lying flat on his stomach
And near him the suspicious gila monster watches
His left ear pressed to the ground is a glass box
Filled with a thunderbolt the artist hasn't forgotten to
    depict above him
The sky-blue balloon shaped like a test-your-strength
    machine at a carnival
When he has to gather the other swans from the horizon
The swan of Montevideo whose wings are spread and
    always ready to beat
Opens two different-colored eyes on the false universe
One of iron sulfate on the trellis of his eyelashes the other
    of diamond-studded mud
He sees the great hexagonal funnel where the machines
    that mankind works nonstop
To cover with bandages will soon be ground to pieces
With his radium candle he rekindles the fire at the bottom
    of the human crucible
Sex of feathers brain of oiled paper
He presides over doubly nocturnal ceremonies whose
    purpose is a fiery extraction that exchanges the hearts
    of men and birds

J'ai accès près de lui en qualité de convulsionnaire
Les femmes ravissantes qui m'introduisent dans le wagon capitonné de roses
Où un hamac qu'elles ont pris soin de me faire de leurs chevelures m'est réservé
De toute éternité
Me recommandent avant de partir de ne pas prendre froid dans la lecture du journal
Il paraît que la statue près de laquelle le chiendent de mes terminaisons nerveuses
Arrive à destination est accordée chaque nuit comme un piano

I'm allowed near him because of the fits I have as a
convulsionary
The ravishing women who show me into the train car
that's upholstered in roses
Where a hammock that they've thoughtfully made me out
of their hair has been reserved for me
For all eternity
They advise me before leaving not to catch a chill reading
the newspaper
It seems that the statue near where the twitch-grass of my
nerve endings
Arrives at its destination is tuned each night like a piano

VIOLETTE NOZIÈRES

(1933)

VIOLETTE NOZIÈRES

(1933)

Tous les rideaux du monde tirés sur tes yeux
Ils auront beau
Devant leur glace à perdre haleine
Tendre l'arc maudit de l'ascendance et de la descendance
Tu ne ressembles plus à personne de vivant ni de mort
Mythologique jusqu'au bout des ongles
Ta prison est la bouée à laquelle ils s'efforcent d'atteindre dans leur sommeil
Tous y reviennent elle les brûle

Comme on remonte à la source d'un parfum dans la rue
Ils dévident en cachette ton itinéraire
La belle écolière du lycée Fénelon qui élevait des chauves-souris dans son pupitre
Le perce-neige du tableau noir
Regagne le logis familial où s'ouvre
Une fenêtre morale dans la nuit
Les parents une fois de plus se saignent pour leur enfant
On a mis le couvert sur la table d'opération
Le brave homme est noir pour plus de vraisemblance
Mécanicien dit-on de trains présidentiels
Dans un pays de pannes où le chef suprême de l'État
Lorsqu'il ne voyage pas à pied de peur des bicyclettes
N'a rien de plus pressé que de tirer le signal d'alarme pour aller s'ébattre en chemise sur le talus
L'excellente femme a lu Corneille dans le livre de classe de sa fille
Femme française et l'a compris

All the curtains in the world drawn before your eyes
It's pointless for them
To stretch the jinxed bow of ancestry and posterity
In front of their mirror gasping for breath
You no longer look like anyone living or dead
Mythological to the tips of your fingernails
Your prison is the buoy they're straining to reach in their sleep
They all come back to it it burns them

As we trace a perfume in the street to its source
They secretly reel off your route
The pretty little schoolgirl from the Lycée Fénelon who raised bats in her desk
The snow-drop of the blackboard
Returns to the family dwelling where
A window of morality opens in the darkness
The parents once more sweat blood for their child
They've laid out the plates on the operating table
The good man is black for more reasons than verisimilitude
An engineer they say on the presidential trains
In a nation of breakdowns where the Chief Executive
When he isn't traveling on foot for fear of bicycles
Has nothing more urgent to do than pull the emergency cord so he can go frolicking on the embankment with only his shirt on
This wonderful wife has read Corneille in her daughter's texts
And retained it too as a good Frenchman expects

Comme son appartement comprend un singulier cabinet de débarras
Où brille mystérieusement un linge
Elle n'est pas de celles qui glissent en riant vingt francs dans leur bas
Le billet de mille cousu dans l'ourlet de sa jupe
Lui assure une rigidité pré-cadavérique
Les voisins sont contents
Tout autour de la terre
Contents d'être les voisins

L'histoire dira
Que M. Nozières était un homme prévoyant
Non seulement parce qu'il avait économisé cent soixante-cinq mille francs
Mais surtout parce qu'il avait choisi pour sa fille un prénom dans la première partie duquel on peut démêler psychanalytiquement son programme
La bibliothèque de chevet je veux dire la table de nuit
N'a plus après cela qu'une valeur d'illustration

Mon père oublie quelquefois que je suis sa fille
L'éperdu
Ce qui tout à la fois craint et rêve de se trahir
Mots couverts comme une agonie sur la mousse
Celui qui dit les avoir entendus de ta bouche brave tout ce qui vaut la peine d'être bravé
Cette sorte de courage est aujourd'hui le seul

The way her apartment holds a strange storage closet
Where a linen sheet mysteriously shines
She isn't the type who laughs as she slips twenty francs in her stocking
The thousand franc note sewn into the hem of her skirt
Assures her a pre-rigor mortis
The neighbors are happy
All over the world
Happy to be neighbors

History will say
That Mister Nozières was a provident man
Not only because he'd saved one hundred and sixty-five thousand francs
But especially because he'd chosen a name for his daughter whose sound allows us to psychoanalytically unravel his plan
After that his bedside library I mean his night table
Has nothing but illustrative value

Sometimes my father forgets that I'm his daughter
The bewildered man
All at once afraid and dreaming of betraying himself
Hints like a death agony on moss
The one who claims to have heard them from your mouth braves everything worth the pain of being braved
That courage is the only kind that exists today

Il nous dédommage à lui seul de cette ruée vers une
tonnelle de capucines
Qui n'existe plus
Tonnelle belle comme un cratère

Mais quel secours
Un autre homme à qui tu faisais part de ta détresse
Dans un lit un homme qui t'avait demandé le plaisir
Le don toujours incomparable de la jeunesse
Il a reçu ta confidence parmi tes caresses
Fallait-il que ce passant fût obscur
Vers toi n'a su faire voler qu'une gifle dans la nuit
blanche

Ce que tu fuyais
Tu ne pouvais le perdre que dans les bras du hasard
Qui rend si flottantes les fins d'après-midi de Paris autour
des femmes aux yeux de cristal fou
Livrées au grand désir anonyme
Auquel fait merveilleusement uniquement
Silencieusement écho
Pour nous le nom que ton père t'a donné et ravi

On glisse où s'est posé ton haut talon de sucre

Tout est égal qu'ils fassent ou non semblant de ne pas
en convenir
Devant ton sexe ailé comme une fleur des Catacombes

In itself it pays us back for that attack upon an arbor of
nasturtiums
That no longer exists
An arbor as beautiful as a shell crater

But what to do
Another man you shared your troubles with
In a bed a man who'd asked you for pleasure
The forever incomparable gift of youth
He took your secret along with your caresses
Did this stranger have to be unknown
To you only knew how to slap your face in the white night

What you ran away from
You could lose only in the arms of chance
Which makes the ends of Paris afternoons drift around
women with mad crystal eyes
Given over to the great anonymous desire
That makes the name your father gave you and violated
Echo for us
Marvelously exclusively silently

We slip where your sugary high heel has landed
Everyone's the same whether they pretend to deny it or not
Before your wingéd sex like a flower from the Catacombs

Étudiants vieillards journalistes pourris faux révolutionnaires prêtres juges
Avocats branlants
Ils savent bien que toute hiérarchie finit là

Pourtant un jeune homme t'attendait énigmatique à une terrasse de café
Ce jeune homme qui au Quartier Latin vendait paraît-il entre-temps l'*Action française*
Cesse d'être mon ennemi puisque tu l'aimais
Vous auriez pu vivre ensemble bien qu'il soit si difficile de vivre avec son amour
Il t'écrivait en partant *Vilaine chérie*
C'est encore joli
Jusqu'à plus ample informé l'argent enfantin n'est que l'écume de la vague

Longtemps après la cavalerie et la chevalerie des chiens
Violette
La rencontre ne sera plus poétiquement qu'une femme seule dans les bosquets introuvables du champ-de-Mars
Assise les jambes en X sur une chaise jaune

Students old men corrupt journalists phony revolutionaries
priests judges
Doddering lawyers
They know all too well that the whole hierarchy ends there

And yet an enigmatic young man waited for you at a sidewalk
café
This young man who in the meantime it seems was selling
Action Française in the Latin Quarter
Stops being my enemy because you loved him
You should have been able to live together though it's so hard
to live with his love
Just as he was leaving he wrote to you *My nasty little sweetie*
It's still pretty
Until we know more about it the childish money is only a fleck
of foam on the wave

When the cavalry and the chivalry of dogs is long gone
Violette
All your meeting will amount to poetically is a woman alone
in the hidden groves of the Champ-de-Mars
Seated with her legs in an X on a yellow chair

L'AIR DE L'EAU

(1934)

THE AIR OF THE WATER

(1934)

Monde dans un baiser
Le joueur à baguettes de coudrier cousues sur les manches
Apaise un essaim de jeunes singes-lions
Descendus à grand fracas de la corniche
Tout devient opaque je vois passer le carrosse de la nuit
Traîné par les axolotls à souliers bleus
Entrée scintillante de la voie de fait qui mène au tombeau
Pavé de paupières avec leurs cils
La loi du talion use un peuple d'étoiles
Et tu te diapres pour moi d'une rosée noire
Tandis que les effrayantes bornes mentales
A cheveux de vigne
Se fendent dans le sens de la longueur
Livrant passage à des aigrettes
Qui regagnent le lac voisin
Les barreaux du spectacle sont merveilleusement tordus
Un long fuseau d'air atteste seul la fuite de l'homme
Au petit matin dans les luzernes illustres
L'heure
N'est plus que ce que sonnent les pièces d'or de la bohémienne
Aux volants de coréopsis

World in a kiss
The drummer with dowsing rods sewn to his sleeves
Calms a swarm of young lion monkeys
Who've come down from the cornice in a great
    commotion
Everything turns opaque I see the coach of night go by
Pulled by axolotls in blue shoes
Sparkling entrance of the path of violence leading to the
    tomb
Paved with eyelids and their lashes
An eye for an eye consumes a nation of stars
And you sprinkle yourself with a black dew for me
While terrifying mental milestones
With vines for hair
Crack apart lengthwise
Making way for egrets
Coming back to the nearby lake
The prison bars on the scene are wonderfully twisted
A long spindle of air gives lone testimony to the man's
    escape
At daybreak in the illustrious alfalfa
The hour
Is no more than the jingling gold coins of the gypsy
    woman
With coreopsis flounces

Une écuyère debout sur un cheval au galop pommelé
de boules d'orage
De loin les bras sont toujours en extension latérale
Le losange poudreux du dessous me rappelle
La tente décorée de bisons bleus
Par les Indiens de l'oreiller
Dehors l'air essaye les gants de gui
Sur un comptoir d'eau pure
Monde dans un baiser monde
A moi les écailles
Les écailles de la grande tortue céleste à ventre
d'hydrophile
Qui se bat chaque nuit dans l'amour
Avec la grande tortue noire le gigantesque scolopendre
de racines

A rider standing on a galloping horse dappled by globes
of storm
At a distance her arms are always stretched out sideways
From below the dusty diamond shape reminds me of
The tent decorated with blue bisons
By the pillow Indians
Outside the air tries on mistletoe gloves
At a counter of pure water
World in a kiss world
For me shells
Shells of the great heavenly turtle with a water beetle's
belly
That fights every night as it makes love
With the great black turtle the gigantic centipede of roots

Le poisson-télescope casse des pierres au fond des livres
Et le plaisir roule ces pierres
Comme vont à dos d'âne de très jeunes filles d'autrefois
En robes d'acacia
Le temps est si clair que je tremble qu'il ne finisse
Un coup de vent sur tes yeux et je ne te verrais plus
Déjà tous les récifs ont pris le large
Les derniers réverbères de paille reculent devant les éteigneurs
Auxquels des papillons blancs font un casque de scaphandriers
Ils ne se risqueront pas dans la ville aux grands chardons
Où souffle un vent blond à décorner les lucanes
J'habite au cœur d'un de ces chardons
Où tes cheveux sont des poignées de portes sous-marines
Des anses à saisir les trésors
Nous pouvons aller et venir sans les pièces frissonnantes
Sans crainte errer dans la forêt de jets d'eau
Nous perdre dans l'immense spath d'Islande
Ta chair arrosée de l'envol de mille oiseaux de paradis
Est une haute flamme couchée dans la neige
La neige de t'avoir trouvée
La descente de lit de loup blanc à perte de vue

The telescope-fish cracks stones at the bottom of books
And pleasure rolls these stones along
Like very young girls of another time riding a donkey
In acacia dresses
This weather is so clear I tremble that it might end
A gust of wind on your eyes and I wouldn't see you any
more
All the reefs have already put out to sea
The last straw streetlamps shrink from the lamplighters
For whom white moths make a diver's helmet
They won't take chances in the city with its huge thistles
Where a blond wind blows hard enough to pull out a stag-
beetle's horns
I live at the heart of one of those thistles
Where your tresses are knobs on undersea doors
Handles for grabbing the treasures
We can come and go without quivering coins
Fearlessly wandering in the forest of fountains
Losing ourselves in the vast Iceland spar
Your flesh splashed by the takeoffs of a thousand birds of
paradise
Is a tall flame lying in the snow
The snow of having found you
The bedside rug of white wolf as far as the eye can see

Je rêve je te vois superposée indéfiniment à toi-même
Tu es assise sur le haut tabouret de corail
Devant ton miroir toujours à son premier quartier
Deux doigts sur l'aile d'eau du peigne
Et en même temps
Tu reviens de voyage tu t'attardes la dernière dans la grotte
Ruisselante d'éclairs
Tu ne me reconnais pas
Tu es étendue sur le lit tu t'éveilles ou tu t'endors
Tu t'éveilles où tu t'es endormie ou ailleurs
Tu es nue la balle de sureau rebondit encore
Mille balles de sureau bourdonnent au-dessus de toi
Si légères qu'à chaque instant ignorées de toi
Ton souffle ton sang sauvés de la folle jonglerie de l'air
Tu traverses la rue les voitures lancées sur toi ne sont plus que leur ombre
Et la même
Enfant
Prise dans un soufflet de paillettes
Tu sautes à la corde
Assez longtemps pour qu'apparaisse au haut de l'escalier invisible
Le seul papillon vert qui hante les sommets de l'Asie

I dream I see you endlessly superimposed upon yourself
You're sitting on the high coral stool
In front of your mirror always in its first quarter
Two fingers on the water wing of your comb
And at the same time
You're returning from a journey you're lingering the last one left in the grotto
Streaming with lightning
You don't recognize me
You're stretched out on the bed you wake up or you fall asleep
You wake up where you went to sleep or somewhere else
You're naked the elderberry ball bounces again
A thousand elderberry balls hum above you
So light that at each instant you're unaware of them
Your breath your blood saved from the crazy juggling of the air
You cross the street the cars hurled at you are nothing but their shadows
And as a
Little girl
Caught in a bellows of sparkles
You jump rope
Long enough so that the one green butterfly that haunts the peaks of Asia

Je caresse tout ce qui fut toi
Dans tout ce qui doit l'être encore
J'écoute siffler mélodieusement
Tes bras innombrables
Serpent unique dans tous les arbres
Tes bras au centre desquels tourne le cristal de la rose
des vents
Ma fontaine vivante de Sivas

Can appear at the top of the invisible stairway
I caress everything that was you
In everything that's yet to be you
I hear the melodious hissing
Of your limitless limbs
The one serpent in all the trees
Your arms at whose center the crystal of the compass rose
turns
My living fountain of Shivas

L'aigle sexuel exulte il va dorer la terre encore une fois
Son aile descendante
Son aile ascendante agite imperceptiblement les manches de la menthe poivrée
Et tout l'adorable déshabillé de l'eau
Les jours sont comptés si clairement
Que le miroir a fait place à une nuée de frondes
Je ne vois du ciel qu'une étoile
Il n'y a plus autour de nous que le lait décrivant son ellipse vertigineuse
D'où la molle intuition aux paupières d'agate œillée
Se soulève parfois pour piquer la pointe de son ombrelle dans la boue de la lumière électrique
Alors des étendues jettent l'ancre se déploient au fond de mon œil fermé
Icebergs rayonnant des coutumes de tous les mondes à venir
Nés d'une parcelle de toi d'une parcelle inconnue et glacée qui s'envole
Ton existence le bouquet géant qui s'échappe de mes bras
Est mal liée elle creuse les murs déroule les escaliers des maisons
Elle s'effeuille dans les vitrines de la rue
Aux nouvelles je pars sans cesse aux nouvelles

The sexual eagle exults it's going to gild the earth again
Its wing coming down
Its wing going up imperceptibly stirs the sleeves of the
peppermint
And the water's whole adorable negligee
The days are reckoned so clearly
That the mirror's made way for a cloud of fronds
All I see of the sky is a star
Nothing around us but milk describing its dizzying ellipse
From where slack intuition with eye-agate lids
Rises now and then to jab the tip of its parasol in the
electric light's mud
Then vast expanses drop anchor unfurl at the bottom of
my closed eyes
Icebergs beaming the customs of all worlds to come
Born from a particle of you from an unknown frozen
particle flying away
Your existence the giant bouquet breaking free of my arms
Is badly tied it bores through walls unwinds the stairways
of houses
It sheds its petals in the shop windows of the street
The news I'm always going in search of the news

Le journal est aujourd'hui de verre et si les lettres
n'arrivent plus
C'est parce que le train a été mangé
La grande incision de l'émeraude qui donna naissance
au feuillage
Est cicatrisée pour toujours les scieries de neige
aveuglante
Et les carrières de chair bourdonnent seules au premier
rayon
Renversé dans ce rayon
Je prends l'empreinte de la mort et de la vie
A l'air liquide

Today's newspaper is glass and if letters don't arrive any more
It's because the train's been eaten
The large incision in the emerald that gave birth to foliage
Is scarred forever the sawmills of blinding snow
And the quarries of flesh are buzzing all alone in the first beam of light
Amazed in this beam
I take the impression of death and life
From the liquid air

Le marquis de Sade a regagné l'intérieur du volcan
en éruption
D'où il était venu
Avec ses belles mains encore frangées
Ses yeux de jeune fille
Et cette raison à fleur de sauve-qui-peut qui ne fut
Qu'à lui
Mais du salon phosphorescent à lampes de viscères
Il n'a cessé de jeter les ordres mystérieux
Qui ouvrent une brèche dans la nuit morale
C'est par cette brèche que je vois
Les grandes ombres craquantes la vieille écorce minée
Se dissoudre
Pour me permettre de t'aimer
Comme le premier homme aima la première femme
En toute liberté
Cette liberté
Pour laquelle le feu même s'est fait homme
Pour laquelle le marquis de Sade défia les siècles de ses
grands arbres abstraits
D'acrobates tragiques
Cramponnés au fil de la Vierge du désir

The Marquis de Sade has gone back inside the erupting
volcano
That he came from
With his beautiful hands still fringed
His girlish eyes
And that every-man-for-himself intellect which was
His alone
But from his phosphorescent study with its lamps of
viscera
He hasn't stopped flinging the mysterious commands
That crack open the darkness of morality
It's through that crack I see
The great creaking shadows the old mined-out husk
Dissolve
So that I can love you
The way the first man loved the first woman
In total freedom
The freedom
For which fire itself became man
For which thc Marquis de Sade defied the centuries with
his great abstract trees
Of tragic acrobats
Clinging to the Virgin gossamer of desire

J'ai devant moi la fée du sel
Dont la robe brodée d'agneaux
Descend jusqu'à la mer
Et dont le voile de chute en chute irise toute la montagne
Elle brille au soleil comme un lustre d'eau vive
Et les petits potiers de la nuit se sont servis de ses ongles sans lune
Pour compléter le service à café de la belladone
Le temps se brouille miraculeusement derrière ses souliers d'étoiles de neige
Tout le long d'une trace qui se perd dans les caresses de deux hermines
Les dangers rétrospectifs ont beau être richement répartis
Des charbons mal éteints au prunellier des haies par le serpent corail qui peut passer pour un très mince filet de sang coagulé
Le fond de l'âtre
Est toujours aussi splendidement noir
Le fond de l'âtre où j'ai appris à voir
Et sur lequel danse sans interruption la crêpe à dos de primevères
La crêpe qu'il faut lancer si haut pour la dorer
Celle dont je retrouve le goût perdu

I have the salt fairy in front of me
Whose dress embroidered with lambs
Trails to the sea
And whose veil fall by fall makes the whole mountain
iridescent
She shines in the sun like a chandelier of spring water
And the night's little potters have used her moonless
fingernails
To complete the belladonna's coffee service
The weather's fogging up miraculously behind her snow-
star shoes
All along a trail lost in the caresses of two ermines
Retrospective dangers are lavishly distributed in vain
Coals half-extinguished at the blackthorn of hedges by the
coral snake able to pass for a very slender thread of
coagulated blood
The back of the fireplace
Is always so wonderfully dark
The back of the fireplace where I learned how to see
And where the crêpe with the primrose back dances
uninterruptedly
The crêpe that has to be tossed so high to turn gold
The one whose lost taste I found again

Dans ses cheveux
La crêpe magique le sceau aérien
De notre amour

In her hair
The magic crêpe the airy imprint
Of our love

Au beau demi-jour de 1934
L'air était une splendide rose couleur de rouget
Et la forêt quand je me préparais à y entrer
Commençait par un arbre à feuilles de papier à cigarettes
Parce que je t'attendais
Et que si tu te promènes avec moi
N'importe où
Ta bouche est volontiers la nielle
D'où repart sans cesse la roue bleue diffuse et brisée qui
monte
Blêmir dans l'ornière
Tous les prestiges se hâtaient à ma rencontre
Un écureuil était venu appliquer son ventre blanc sur
mon cœur
Je ne sais comment il se tenait
Mais la terre était pleine de reflets plus profonds que
ceux de l'eau
Comme si le métal eût enfin secoué sa coque
Et toi couchée sur l'effroyable mer de pierreries
Tu tournais
Nue
Dans un grand soleil de feu d'artifice
Je te voyais descendre lentement des radiolaires
Les coquilles même de l'oursin j'y étais
Pardon je n'y étais déjà plus

In the beautiful half-light of 1934
The air was a splendid pink the color of red mullet
And the forest when I prepared to enter it
Began with a tree with cigarette paper leaves
Because I was waiting for you
And if you come for a walk with me
No matter where
Your mouth is the incredible all-spice
From which the blue wheel diffuse and broken endlessly
    sets out and rises
Turning pale in the rut
All the marvels hurried to meet me
A squirrel had come to press its white belly against my
    heart
I don't know how he made himself do it
But the earth was filled with reflections deeper than those
    in water
As if metal had finally shaken off its shell
And you lying on the frightening ocean of precious gems
Were turning
Naked
In a huge sun of fireworks
I saw you slowly evolving from the radiolarians
Even the shells of the sea urchins I was there
Wait a minute I wasn't there any more

J'avais levé la tête car le vivant écrin de velours blanc
m'avait quitté
Et j'étais triste
Le ciel entre les feuilles luisait hagard et dur comme
une libellule
J'allais fermer les yeux
Quand les deux pans du bois qui s'étaient brusquement
écartés s'abattirent
Sans bruit
Comme les deux feuilles centrales d'un muguet immense
D'une fleur capable de contenir toute la nuit
J'étais où tu me vois
Dans le parfum sonné à toute volée
Avant qu'elles ne revinssent comme chaque jour à la
vie changeante
J'eus le temps de poser mes lèvres
Sur tes cuisses de verre

I had raised my head because the living jewel box of white velvet had left me
And I was sad
The sky between the leaves was shining haggard and hard like a dragonfly
I was going to shut my eyes
When two wooden booms that had suddenly swung apart came crashing down
Without a sound
Like the two center leaves of an immense lily-of-the-valley
Of a flower capable of containing the whole night
I was where you see me now
In the set-all-the-bells-a-ringing perfume
Before they could return as they do each day to fickle life
I just had time to place my lips
On your glass thighs

Yeux zinzolins de la petite Babylonienne trop blanche
Au nombril sertissant une pierre de même couleur
Quand s'ouvre comme une croisée sur un jardin nocturne
La main de Jacqueline X
Que vous êtes pernicieux au fond de cette main
Yeux d'outre-temps à jamais humides
Fleur qui pourriez vous appeler la réticence du prophète
C'en est fait du présent du passé de l'avenir
Je chante la lumière unique de la coïncidence
La joie de m'être penché sur la grande rosace du glacier
supérieur
Les infiltrations merveilleuses dont on s'aperçoit
un beau jour qu'elles ont fait un cornet du plancher
La portée des incidents étranges mais insignifiants
à première vue
Et leur don d'appropriation finale vertigineuse à
moi-même
Je chante votre horizon fatal
Vous qui clignez imperceptiblement dans la main de
mon amour
Entre le rideau de vie
Et le rideau de cœur
Yeux zinzolins
YZ
De l'alphabet secret de la toute-nécessité

Zinnia-red eyes of the too white little Babylonian girl
With the navel bearing a stone of the same color
When the hand of Jacqueline X
Opens like a casement window on a garden at night
How pernicious you are at the bottom of that hand
Eyes beyond time forever moist
Flower that could be called The Prophet's Reticence
The present the past the future are finished
I sing the one light of coincidence
The joy of leaning over the big rose window of the upper glacier
The marvelous seepage that one fine day you notice has changed the wood floor into a cornet
The meaning of occurrences that are strange but at first glance insignificant
And their gift of total possession dizzying for me
I sing your fateful horizon
You winking imperceptibly in my love's hand
Between the curtain of life
And the curtain of heart
Your zinnia-red eyes
YZ
Of the secret alphabet of absolute necessity

Il allait être cinq heurs du matin
La barque de buée tendait sa chaîne à faire éclater les vitres
Et dehors
Un ver luisant
Soulevait comme une feuille Paris
Ce n'était qu'un cri tremblant continu
Un cri parti de l'hospice de la Maternité tout proche
FINIS FONDEUR FOU
Mais tout ce qui passait de joie dans l'exhalaison de cette douleur
Il me semble que j'étais tombé longtemps
J'avais encore la main crispée sur une poignée d'herbes
Et soudain ce froissement de fleurs et d'aiguilles de glace
Ces sourcils verts ce balancier d'étoile filante
De quelles profondeurs pouvait bien remonter la cloche
Hermétique
Dont rien la veille encore ne me faisait prévoir l'arrêt à ce palier
La cloche aux parois de laquelle
Ondine
Tout en agitant pour t'élever la pédale du sagittaire en fer de lance
Tu avais gravé les signes infaillibles
De mon enchantement

It was going on five in the morning
The ship of steam stretched its chain to shatter the
    windows
And outside
A glowworm
Lifted Paris like a leaf
It was only a long trembling scream
A scream from the Maternity Hospital nearby
FINIS FOUNDRY FANATIC
But whatever joy escaped in the exhalation of that pain
It seems to me that I was falling for a long time
I still had my fist clenched around a handful of grass
And suddenly that rustle of flowers and needles of ice
Those green eyebrows that shooting-star pendulum
From what depths was the bell actually able to rise again
The hermetic bell
Which nothing last night made me foresee would stop on
    this landing
The bell whose sides read
Undinc
Moving to raise your spearheaded Sagittarius pedal
You had carved the infallible signs
Of my enchantment

Au moyen d'un poignard dont le manche de corail
bifurque à l'infini
Pour que ton sang et le mien
N'en fassent qu'un

With a dagger whose coral handle forks into infinity
So that your blood and mine
Would become one

Ils vont tes membres déployant autour de toi des draps verts
Et le monde extérieur
En pointillé
Ne joue plus les prairies ont déteint les jours des clochers se rejoignent
Et le puzzle social
A livré sa dernière combinaison
Ce matin encore ces draps se sont levés ont fait voile avec toi d'un lit prismatique
Dans le château brouillé du saule aux yeux de lama
Pour lequel la tête en bas
Je suis parti jadis
Draps amande de ma vie
Quand tu marches le cuivre de Vénus
Innerve la feuille glissante et sans bords
Ta grande aile liquide
Bat dans le chant des vitriers

Your arms and legs they move around you unfolding green
sheets
And the world outside
All stippled
Doesn't play anymore the fields have washed the color
from the days steeples intersect again
And the social puzzle
Has yielded its last solution
Once again this morning these sheets got up and set sail
with you from a prismatic bed
In the jumbled castle of the llama-eyed willow
That I set out for a long time ago
My head upside-down
Sheets almond of my life
When you walk the trumpet of Venus
Excites the nerves of the gliding rimless leaf
Your great fluid wing
Beats in the glassmakers' song

Et mouvement encore
Mouvement rythmé par le pilage de coquilles d'huître et d'étoiles rousses
Dans les tapas des îles heureuses
Je pense à un très ancien livre de voyages
Où l'on conte qu'un marin abandonné dans l'une de ces îles
S'était épris si éperdument d'une indigène
Et s'en était fait si éperdument aimer
Qu'ils parvenaient à échanger sur toutes choses des impressions parfois très subtiles
Au moyen d'un langage unique de caresses
Lorsque je te vois je retrouve en moi cet homme qui avait oublié trop volontiers la parole
Et je souris lorsqu'un ami me reproche non sans raison
De ne pas avoir en général
Montré assez de défiance à l'égard de cette obsession poétique
Il dit même de cette fausse intuition tyrannique
Que serait la nostalgie de l'âge d'or
Mais les événements modernes ne sont pas forcément dépouillés de tout sens originel et final
Et la rencontre
Élective vraiment comme elle peut être
De l'homme et de la femme

And again motion
Motion rhythmatized by the grinding of oyster shells and russet stars
In the tapas of happy islands
I think of a very old travel book
Which tells of a sailor abandoned on one of those islands
Who had fallen so hopelessly in love with a native girl
And had made her love him so hopelessly
That they managed to exchange sometimes very subtle impressions about all sorts of things
By means of a unique language of caresses
When I see you I rediscover in me that man who had too willingly forgotten speech
And I smile when a friend reproaches me not without reason
For generally not having
Shown enough distrust with respect to this poetic obsession
He says the same of that false tyrannical intuition
Which might be our nostalgia for the golden age
But modern events aren't necessarily stripped of every original or final meeting
And the meeting
Freely chosen it really can be that way
Of man and woman

Toi que je découvre et qui restes pour moi toujours à découvrir
Les premiers navigateurs à la recherche moins des pays
Que de leur propre cause
Voguent éternellement dans la voix des sirènes
Cette rencontre
Avec tout ce qu'elle comporte à distance de fatal
Cette précipitation l'un vers l'autre de deux systèmes tenus séparément pour subjectifs
Met en branle une série de phénomènes très réels
Qui concourent à la formation d'un monde distinct
De nature à faire honte à ce que nous apercevrions
A son défaut
De celui-ci
La barbarie des civilisations n'y peut rien
Je lisais tout à l'heure dans l'Humanité
Qu'en Oïrotie
Dans une contrée où toutes les jolies filles il y a vingt ans
Étaient vendues aux beys
La femme ayant acquis maintenant le droit de disposer d'elle-même
On avait pu voir
Un jeune homme apporter à une jeune fille un petit bouquet

You whom I discover and who are always there for me to
discover
The first explorers searching less for lands
Than for their own origins
Sail eternally in the sirens' voices
That meeting
With everything fatal which it so distantly involves
That precipitation one toward the other of two systems
considered separately as subjective
Puts into motion a series of very real phenomena
That converge to form a distinct world
Of such a nature as to put to shame whatever we might
perceive
Without it
Against this
The barbarity of civilizations is of no avail
I read a little while ago in L'Humanité
That in the Oirat
In a region where twenty years ago all the pretty girls
Were sold to beys
Now that women have gained the right to decide their
own fate
You could see
A young man bringing a little bouquet to a girl

A ta place je me méfierais du chevalier de paille
Cette espèce de Roger délivrant Angélique
Leitmotiv ici des bouches de métro
Disposées en enfilade dans tes cheveux
C'est une charmante hallucination lilliputienne
Mais le chevalier de paille le chevalier de paille
Te prend en croupe et vous vous jetez dans la haute allée de peupliers
Dont les premières feuilles perdues beurrent les roses morceaux de pain de l'air
J'adore ces feuilles à l'égal
De ce qu'ü y a de suprêmement indépendant en toi
Leur pâle balance
A compter de violettes
Juste ce qu'il faut pour que transparaisse aux plus tendres plis de ton corps
Le message indéchiffrable capital
D'une bouteille qui a longtemps tenu la mer
Et je les adore quand elles se rassemblent comme un coq blanc
Furieux sur le perron du château de la violence
Dans la lumière devenue déchirante où il ne s'agit plus de vivre
Dans le taillis enchanté
Où le chasseur épaule un fusil à crosse de faisan

If I were you I'd watch out for the straw knight
That Ruggiero rescuing Angelica type
Leitmotif of metro exits here
Arranged in succession in your hair
It's a delightful Lilliputian hallucination
But the straw knight the straw knight
Pillions you behind him and you hurl yourselves down the high lane of poplars
Whose first fallen leaves butter the roses the air's bits of bread
I adore these leaves as much
As what is supremely independent in you
Their pallid scales
Weighing the exact number of violets
Just what's needed to make the indecipherable essential message
Of a bottle that's been at sea a long time
Show through your body's tenderest folds
And I adore them when they assemble like a white rooster
Furious on the steps of the castle of violence
In the light grown heartrending where it's no longer a question of living
In the enchanted coppice
Where the hunter shoulders a gun with a pheasant for a stock

Ces feuilles qui sont la monnaie de Danaé
Lorsqu'il m'est donné de t'approcher à ne plus te voir
D'étreindre en toi ce lieu jaune ravagé
Le plus éclatant de ton œil
Où les arbres volent
Où les bâtiments commencent à être secoués d'une
gaîté de mauvais aloi
Où les jeux du cirque se poursuivent avec un luxe
effréné dans la rue
Survivre
Du plus loin deux ou trois silhouettes se détachent
Sur le groupe étroit bat le drapeau parlementaire

These leaves that are the coins of Danaë
When I have the chance to come so close I can no longer
    see you
To embrace in you that yellow ravaged place
Your eyes' most dazzling
Where buildings begin to be shaken by a degraded joy
Where circus tricks follow each other in unchecked
    profusion in the street
To survive
In the farthest distance two or three silhouettes stand out
Against the huddled group the flag of truce flaps

On me dit que là-bas les plages sont noires
De la lave allée à la mer
Et se déroulent au pied d'un immense pic fumant de
    neige
Sous un second soleil de serins sauvages
Quel est donc ce pays lointain
Qui semble tirer toute sa lumière de ta vie
Il tremble bien réel à la pointe de tes cils
Doux à ta carnation comme un linge immatériel
Frais sorti de la malle entrouverte des âges
Derrière toi
Lançant ses derniers feux sombres entre tes jambes
Le sol du paradis perdu
Glace de ténèbres miroir d'amour
Et plus bas vers tes bras qui s'ouvrent
A la preuve par le printemps
D'APRÈS
De l'inexistence du mal
Tout le pommier en fleur de la mer

They tell me the beaches over there are black
From lava gone into the sea
And unroll at the foot of an immense peak fuming with
    snow
Under a second sun of wild canaries
So what faraway country is this
That seems to draw all its light from your life
It trembles so real at the tips of your lashes
As gentle to the pinkness of your flesh as an immaterial
    cloth
Fresh from the half-opened trunk of the ages
Behind you
Hurling its last dark fires between your legs
The ground of the lost paradise
Ice of shadows mirror of love
And lower toward your arms opening
With the proof of spring
AFTER
The nonexistence of evil
The whole blossoming apple tree of the sea

Toujours pour la première fois
C'est à peine si je te connais de vue
Tu rentres à telle heure de la nuit dans une maison
oblique à ma fenêtre
Maison tout imaginaire
C'est là que d'une seconde à l'autre
Dans le noir intact
Je m'attends à ce que se produise une fois de plus la
déchirure fascinante
La déchirure unique
De la façade et de mon cœur
Plus je m'approche de toi
En réalité
Plus la clé chante à la porte de la chambre inconnue
Où tu m'apparais seule
Tu es d'abord tout entière fondue dans le brillant
L'angle fugitif d'un rideau
C'est un champ de jasmin que j'ai contemplé à l'aube
sur une route des environs de Grasse
Avec ses cueilleuses en diagonale
Derrière elles l'aile sombre tombante des plants dégarnis
Devant elles l'équerre de l'éblouissant
Le rideau invisiblement soulevé
Rentrent en tumulte toutes les fleurs

Always for the first time
As if I hardly know what you look like
You come back at a certain time of night to a house at an
    angle to my window
A completely imaginary house
Where from one second to the next
In the unbroken darkness
I expect it to happen again the fascinating ripping
The one and only ripping
Of its façade and my heart
The closer I come to you
In reality
The more the key sings in the door of the unknown room
Where you appear for me all alone
First you are totally fused with the brightness
The fleeting angle of a curtain
It's a field of jasmine I've gazed on at dawn on a road just
    outside
Grasse
With its diagonal of women pickers
Behind them the shadowy falling wing of stripped
    seedlings
In front of them the T-square of dazzlement
The curtain invisibly raised
All the flowers come back in a tumult

C'est toi aux prises avec cette heure trop longue jamais
    assez trouble jusqu'au sommeil
Toi comme si tu pouvais être
La même à cela près que je ne te rencontrerai peut-être
    jamais
Tu fais semblant de ne pas savoir que je t'observe
Merveilleusement je ne suis plus sûr que tu le sais
Ton désœuvrement m'emplit les yeux de larmes
Une nuée d'interprétations entoure chacun de tes gestes
C'est une chasse à la miellée
Il y a des rocking-chairs sur un pont il y a des branchages
    qui risquent de t'égratigner dans la forêt
Il y a dans une vitrine rue Notre-Dame-de-Lorette
Deux belles jambes croisées prises dans de hauts bas
Qui s'évasent au centre d'un grand trèfle blanc
Il y a une échelle de soie déroulée sur le lierre
Il y a
Qu'à me pencher sur le précipice
De la fusion sans espoir de ta présence et de ton absence
J'ai trouvé le secret
De t'aimer
Toujours pour la première fois

It's you in the grip of this long long hour never troubled enough till you fall asleep
You as though you could be
The same except that maybe I'll never meet you
You pretend not to know I watch you
Amazingly I'm no longer sure you know it
Your idleness brings tears to my eyes
A cloud of interpretations surrounds each of your movements
It's a hunt for honeydew
There are rocking chairs on a bridge there are branches trying to scratch you in the forest
In a shop window on the Rue Notre-Dame-de-Lorette there are
Two beautiful crossed legs trapped in long stockings
That flare out at the center of a big white clover
There's
Only for me to lean over the cliff
Of the hopeless fusion of your presence and your absence
I've discovered the secret
Of always loving you
For the first time

AU LAVOIR NOIR

(1936)

IN THE BLACK LAUNDRY SHED

(1936)

Papillons de nuit, petits toits de la nécessité naturelle à l'œil de paille, à l'œil de poutre! Et vous, toits humains qui vous envolez chaque nuit aussi pour revenir vous poser les ailes jointes sous le compas des dernières étoiles : il va falloir vivre encore, quel temps fait-il? De l'intérieur de la maison on découvre en s'éveillant le dessous des ailes, un peu de leur poussière n'a pas encore fini de tomber, elle danse dans le premier rayon de soleil. Et c'est toute la vie d'hier qui se ramifie en un corail impossible de la pâleur de tes mains, cette poudre est le buvard de tes premiers gestes. Les as-tu vus s'élancer à la tombée du jour des arbres et des haies, pour couper les fils télégraphiques qui se roulent en bobines derrière eux et foncer par les fenêtres entrouvertes sur la dragée haute? Un long frisson parcourt aussitôt l'assistance, il est à la fois question de fermer et d'ouvrir; quelqu'un trouve même qu'une odeur suffocante se répand : à bas la myrrhe! Les fusils restent cependant aux murs mais le silence devient intolérable : bien sûr, on entendrait voler un papillon. Les avions se croisent à ce moment dans le ciel, ils descendent même très bas, ils menacent d'atterrir sur la maison sans toit, de faire jacasser les coqs de la vaisselle. Mais nul n'en a cure tant les fleurs du papier s'émeuvent, et l'on redoute d'une seconde à l'autre une pire rafale de grêle. Tout peut apparaître dans un grêlon, la Vierge à des enfants, cela s'est vu, et même un papillon à des hommes. Mais le papillon disparaît beaucoup plus lentement. Dans ce dernier cas tout me porte à croire que je suis coupable, on vient me chercher jusqu'à table, je distingue les menottes, il va me falloir lutter, lutter encore pour être libre! La nuit, quand il n'y a plus de plafond, je sens s'ouvrir sur moi les ailes de la lichénée bleue! Un soir que je parlais plus que de coutume, un grand papillon entra : pris

Moths, little roofs of natural necessity with motes in their eyes, with beams in their eyes! And you, human roofs who also fly away each night to come and place your folded wings beneath the compass of the furthest stars: you're going to have to go on living, what's the weather like? On waking we discover inside the house the underside of the wings, a little of their dust is still falling, it dances in the first ray of sunlight. And it's the life of all days past that branches out into an impossible coral from the paleness of your hands, that powder is the blotter of your first gestures. Have you seen them spring from the trees and hedges at nightfall to cut the telegraph wires that roll up on bobbins behind them and jump through half-open windows for some tidbit? Right away a long shudder travels through the audience, it's closing time and opening time simultaneously; someone even discovers that a suffocating odor is spreading: down with myrrh! Meanwhile the rifles stay on the walls but the silence becomes intolerable: of course, you could hear the flight of a butterfly. At this moment planes pass each other in the sky, they even swoop very low, they threaten to land on the house without a roof, to make the roosters on the dishes chatter. But the paper flowers are so excited that no one notices, and it's feared that any second a worse hailstorm will fall. Anything can appear in a hailstone, the Virgin can appear to children, that's been seen, and even a butterfly can appear to men. But the butterfly disappears much more slowly. In this last instance everything leads me to believe that I'm the guilty one, in fact they track me right to the dinner table, I can make out the handcuffs, I'm going to have to fight, fight again to be free! At night, when the ceiling is gone, I sense the wings of the female blue opening above me. One night when I was talking more than usual, a large butterfly flew in: seized with

d'une terreur indicible à pointe d'émerveillement, comme je lui opposais les grands gestes désordonnés que je croyais appelés à le faire fuir il se posa sur mes lèvres.

LE PAPILLON

Non. La belle bouteille cachetée des mots que tu aimes et qui te font mal doit rester enrobée de tulle et tu risquerais à l'élever trop haut de faire flamber à l'intérieur une rose grise. Une jeune femme en transe, chaque fois que s'enflamme la rose grise, apparaît sur un perron dont les degrés brûlent à leur tour derrière elle et c'est autant de paliers du désir que tu n'atteindras plus. La jeune femme, l'immortelle rose grise à la main, fait le tour de la maison qui descend toujours. C'est seulement quand les murs en ont déjà disparu dans le sol qu'elle retourne s'étendre sur le lit de la chambre qui fut la plus haute et que referme instantanément au-dessus d'elle une coupe fraîche de gazon. Toute la maison, reprise alors en montée par un ascenseur insensible, revient dans l'espace à une position légèrement inférieure à celle qu'elle occupait. Le gazon de plus en plus ras n'est plus, tiré aux quatre points cardinaux, qu'un tamis de gaze verte laissant passer dans la nuit le seul parfum aimanté de la rose grise... Adieu. Je repars sur ma roue oblongue, pareille au désir japonais de se jeter dans la gueule du volcan.

Et le merveilleux petit bâillon vivant reprit sa course, tant qu'il fut dans la pièce suivi comme au projecteur par la lanterne sourde de mon enfance. Mes cils battaient toujours à se rompre et je n'aurais sans doute pas reconnu mon regard épinglé dans une glace en sortant.

an unspeakable terror and even amazement, as I confronted it with big disorderly gestures that I thought I had to use to make it go away, it landed on my lips.

THE BUTTERFLY

No. The beautiful bottle sealed with the words you love and that hurt you must remain wrapped in tulle and by lifting it too high you risk setting fire to a gray rose inside. A young woman in a trance, each time the gray rose starts to burn, appears on a flight of stairs whose steps in turn catch fire behind her and those are all the staircase landings of desire you'll never reach. The young woman, immortal gray rose in hand, makes the rounds of the house that's always sinking. It's only when the walls have already disappeared into the ground that she returns to stretch out on the bed in the room that was at the top and a freshly-mowed lawn instantly shuts over her. The whole house, lifted back up by an imperceptible elevator, resumes its place slightly below the position it used to occupy. The lawn, more and more close-cropped, stretched to the four cardinal points, is nothing more than a sieve of green gauze letting the gray rose's one magnetized perfume drift into the night.... Farewell. I depart again on my oblong wheel, like the Japanese desire to hurl oneself into the volcano's mouth.

And the marvelous live little muzzle started to run again, continuing so long as it was followed around the room as if in the beam of the bull's-eye lantern I had as a child. My eyelashes kept batting like they were going to break and I probably wouldn't have recognized my face pinned in the mirror as I went out. I had been left alone for

Depuis longtemps on m'avait laissé seul. La rue était une table mise avec les couverts bien réguliers de ses lumières, les cristaux de ses voitures filant les éclairs, où cependant, de-ci de-là, le haut d'un buste de femme, rendu lui aussi transparent par la vitesse, mettait l'imperceptible point de phosphorescence laiteuse qui tend à gagner toute l'étendue des verreries de fouille. O substance, m'écriai-je, il faut donc toujours en revenir aux ailes de papillon! Et j'avais, pour ma consolation philosophique, le souvenir de l'homme qui, consulté sur ce qu'il aimerait qu'on fît pour lui quand il viendrait à mourir, demanda qu'on plaçât dans son cercueil une brosse (pour quand il tomberait en poussière). La belle brosse sentimentale court toute seule sur le temps. Jasmins, jasmins des cuisses de ma maîtresse, rappelez à vous l'atropos qui jette un cri strident lorsqu'on le saisit.

Les plus obscurs présages renaissaient. Ils se guidaient sur ce cri lugubre, repris par l'instrument qu'un mendiant cherchait à accorder, un instrument aux ouïes en forme de V. Les étoiles étaient du sel renversé, vite une pincée d'algues sèches par-dessus l'épaule. Le pharmacien, qui s'était fait la tête du peintre Seurat, venait de paraître sur sa porte, tenant manifestement à régner sur la bonne odeur d'iode supplémentaire. Je n'ai jamais compris pourquoi il avait voulu venir flanqué de ses bocaux vert et rouge au Palais des Glaces mais l'effet était superbe. Quand ils furent inespérément teintés à perte de vue, tous les miroirs d'alors se brisèrent en forme de papillons.

a long time. The street was a table laid with the very orderly place settings of its lights, the crystal of its carriages spinning out thunderbolts, where in the meantime, here and there, the top of a woman's bust, also rendered transparent by speed, placed the imperceptible dot of milky phosphorescence that tends to overtake the entire range of excavated glassware. Oh substance, I exclaimed, then must I always come back to the butterfly's wings! And for philosophical consolation I had the memory of the man who, asked what he'd like done for him when his time came to die, requested that a brush be placed in his coffin (for when he'd crumble to dust). The beautiful sentimental brush dashes over time all by itself. Jasmines, jasmines of my mistress' thighs, call for the death's-head moth that lets out a shriek when you grab it.

The most obscure omens were reborn. They were guided by that mournful cry, taken up again by the instrument that a beggar tried to tune, an instrument with its sound holes in a V shape. The stars were spilled salt, quick, a pinch of dried seaweed over your shoulder. The pharmacist, who had turned into the head of the painter Seurat, had just appeared in the doorway, obviously determined to rule over the sweet smell of iodine supplements. I've never understood why he wanted to come to the Ice Palace surrounded by his green and red apothecary jars but the effect was superb. When they were hopelessly tinted as far as the eye can see, all the mirrors of old broke into butterfly shapes.

C'est dans l'un de ces éclats que je me regarde. Tu es dans ta pensée comme sur un talon toujours virant un vol de castagnettes, tu es, te dis-je, dans ton sort, attaché au mauvais diamant rose, le genou de la femme sur quoi, dans l'étourdissement, retombe le volant d'écume admirable. Tu as des mains pour perdre ce que tu n'as pas trouvé. Tu es immobile, enchaîné à la roche froide au-dessus du précipice, en ce point culminant de toute la tragédie où Io passe dans Eschyle, annoncée par la phrase sibylline :

LE CHŒUR

Entends-tu la voix de cette jeune fille-qui-porte-des-cornes-de-vache?

Je l'entends comme je me vois. A ce signe sur sa tête, à cet aiguillon de feu qui la pénètre et qu'elle fuit, je reconnais celle qui répand chaque nuit sa grande plainte voluptueuse sur le monde, je sais la saluer à travers tous ces êtres qui me poursuivent de leurs courbes contrariantes et augurales comme les loups seuls visibles d'un bal masqué. Ce qui fut ne demande encore qu'à s'assombrir dans les yeux de l'Argus aveugle et brillant qui veille toujours. Mais le guidon de plumes ne lance pas en vain contre le lustre de ce que nous rêvons logiquement d'établir la petite machine parfois incendiée, toujours incendiaire. Entends-tu, mais entends-tu, dis-moi, la voix de cette jeune fille… ? Le soleil vient seulement de se coucher.

It's in one of these shards that I'm looking at myself. You're in your thoughts like a heel always knocking over a flight of castanets; I'm telling you, you are in your fate, tied to the flawed pink diamond, the woman's knee resting where, to her astonishment, the admirable flounce of foam breaks again. You have hands for losing what you haven't found. You're motionless, chained to the cold rock above the cliff, at the climax of the whole tragedy where Io appears in Aeschylus, announced by the sibylline sentence:

CHORUS

Do you hear the voice of that girl-with-the-cow-horns?

I hear it the way I see myself. By the sign on her head, by the pricking fire that goads her on, that she's running from, I recognize the one who spreads her great voluptuous lament over the world each night, I know how to salute her through all the beings who pursue me with their irritating and prophetic curves like the dominoes you can only see at a masked ball. What was asks only to cloud over in the eyes of the blind and shining Argus who stays awake always. Not in vain does the pennant of feathers hurl the little machine, sometimes on fire, always incendiary, against the chandelier of what we logically dream of constructing. Can you hear it, can you hear it, well, tell me, the voice of that young girl…? The sun has only just set.

NOTES

[Arabic numbers refer to lines in poems or to pages in prose texts. Uncredited translations are by B.Z. and Z.R.]

•

Cover: The cover of this book features a detail from André Breton's photomontage *L'écriture automatique [Automatic writing]* (ca. 1938). The original shows the words "L'écriture automatique," most likely in Breton's handwriting, below the image. The head was apparently taken from a photograph made during Breton's schooldays, and the woman smiling from behind the bars is the American actress Phyllis Haver in a still from the 1927 film production of *Chicago,* also the source of the more recent Broadway musical and film.

In 2002 a Sotheby's auction in Paris sold many manuscripts and books from the vast collection of Pierre Leroy. One of them was Paul Éluard's copy of the first (1930) edition of his and Breton's collaborative text *L'Immaculée conception / The Immaculate Conception.* Éluard sent it to the bookbinder Paul Bonet who created for the poet a special version that "included additional, original material closely associated with its earlier publication, including 'collage portraits of the two writers by Breton'" (Colin Gleadell, *The Guardian,* June 24, 2002). Our cover derives from the self-portrait photocollage made by Breton and given to Éluard sometime after the publication of *L'Immaculée conception* and that is now part of this special volume created by Paul Bonet. The first appearance of the Breton photomontage seems to have been in Breton and Éluard's *Dictionnaire abrégé du surrealisme* (1938), where it appears in Breton's entry. In addition, Breton added a biographical poem to it:

Jugement de l'auteur sur lui-mème

Héraclite mourant, Pierre de lune,
Sade, le cyclone à tète de grain
de millet, le tamanoir: non plus
grand désir eût été d'appartenir
à la famille des grands indésirables.

André Breton

The author's self-judgment

Heraclitus dying, moonstone,
Sade, the cyclone with the birdseed
head, the giant anteater: no greater
ambition than to belong
to the family of the great undesirables.

André Breton

PAWNSHOP [MONT DE PIÉTÉ] (1919)

The *"mont de piété"* is the traditional French name for a pawnshop, but the literal image that it presents is of a "mountain of piety." Nothing of this image resides in our English word.

Breton is using "borrowed" *materia poetica* in a number of these poems, a practice encouraged by the collage esthetic of the cubists and dadaists and soon to form a cornerstone of Surrealist practice. The title also suggests that *Pawnshop* is a potpourri of techniques and stylistic influences—Mallarmé, Rimbaud, the *symboliste* poets, and Apollinaire, among them—and that in these poems Breton is both acknowledging and piously "redeeming" his literary debts. The oddities and curiosities to be found in a pawnshop also prefigure the Surrealist penchant for discovering the "marvelous" in everyday life.

See the *Oeuvres Vol. I* (1065–1098) for a running discussion of Breton's prosody, especially the employment of the truncated alexandrine line in many of these poems.

"WAY" ["FAÇON"]

Originally the epigraph *"Chéruit."* headed the poem. It was the name of a *maison de couture* on the Place Vendôme in Paris whose owner, Madeleine Chéruit (1863–1955), became one of the trendsetters in women's fashion. In 1930 Breton annotated a set of proofs of *Mont de piété*. There he mentioned the "countless fashion magazines that [he] reveled in at the time." (During World War I, from 1916–17, Breton was stationed in Nantes, where "Way" was composed.) The editors of the *Oeuvres I* see this distraction as another "way" (*"Façon"*) that the young poet Breton devised to negate the impact of the war (*Oeuvres I*, 1073).

12: "La Cour Batave": La Cour Batave was a lingerie shop in the Porte Saint-Denis neighborhood. When in 1918 the German gun "Big Bertha" dropped a shell on the center of Paris, Aragon noted the following: "At the moment of the explosion that I'm talking about, Breton found himself not very far from what was formerly the Cour des Miracles, on the Rue Réaumur, and saw the large windows of the shop at La Cour Batave crack from top to bottom...; one of the first poems that my new friend showed me when we met in 1917 was 'Way,' written in 1916, which André felt very strongly about..." (*Oeuvres I*, 1073). For Aragon see the note, below, to "Five Dreams" [IV]. Also, see the note to "Sunflower" for another cxample of the "prophetic" element in Breton's poetry. Batavia was also the Dutch name for Jakarta, Indonesia. Rimbaud arrived there as a soldier in the Dutch army in July 1876, when the colony was known as Java; he was then nearly twenty-four years of age. He would desert a month later, perhaps also from Batavia.

"AGE" ["AGE"]

This prose poem distinctly shows the influence of the Rimbaud of *Les Illuminations,* whose "Aube"/ "Dawn" concludes: "Dawn and the child fell to the bottom of the wood. When I awoke, it was noon" (*Illuminations,* Ashbery translation, 101).

last line: "staircase landings": Staircases, flights of steps, and staircase landings were an obsession of the poet and may be encountered in thirteen of the poems in this anthology of his work, including "Five Dreams," "Silhouette of Straw," "The Pink Death," and "Unconscious."

date: February 19, 1916, was Breton's twentieth birthday.

"GROUSE" ["COQS DE BRUYÈRE"]

3: "*quetsch*": *Quetsche* is an Alsatian term for a kind of plum. *Quetsch* is a dry white Alsatian brandy distilled from its juice. *Quetschen* (G.) means "to squeeze, crush, flatten," and relates to other verbs meaning "to strike (against), injure, wound, break up."

Is Breton referring to the color of the helmets or uniforms worn by German soldiers in World War I?

7: "Bengal lights": A kind of firework or flare producing a steady and vivid blue-colored light, used for signals. It appeared extensively in the trench warfare of World War I. Soldiers assigned to install barbed wire "lived in constant fear of enemy flares, sent up to illuminate an area of the battlefield as if by daylight. Men caught in No Man's Land by such flares would either freeze until the light of the flare died, or else (more often) throw themselves instantly to the ground" (See "Wiring Parties," http://www.firstworldwar.com/atoz/wiring.htm).

8: "the Tyrol": An alpine region distributed over Austria, Italy, and Switzerland. The Trentino frontier was the scene of ferocious fighting from late 1915 to the end of World War I. This poem may incorporate the language of shell-shocked combatants whom Breton treated as an army medical officer.

14: "nasturtiums": In his 1930 annotations to *Mont de piété,* Breton said that "A letter from Nantes really contained nasturtiums." The editors of the *Oeuvres I* suggest that a love affair in Nantes lies at the origins of the poem (1079).

"ANDRÉ DERAIN" ["ANDRÉ DERAIN"]

Title: André Derain (1880–1954) was a French fauvist painter. He contributed two drawings for the original edition of *Mont de piété*. In his 1930 notes Breton remembered "thinking especially about [Derain's painting] *Saturday,* the photographic reproduction of which I cut out of *Les Soirées de Paris* and kept with me all throughout the war." The editors of the *Oeuvres I* add that some of the elements of the painting appear—albeit obliquely—in the poem. (*Oeuvres I*, 1083–84.)

4: "spur": Here, a slender, usually hollow projection from some part of a flower.

20: "almah": Almah is a Hebrew word meaning a young woman of childbearing age who has not yet had a child, and who may be an unmarried virgin or married young woman. See Rimbaud's poem, *"Est-elle almée?"* (*"Is she an almah?"*).

22: "cornette": The large white hat worn by the Daughters of Charity. Also spelled "cornet" and "coronet." The headpiece was officially abandoned by the order in 1964.

23: "coif": A close-fitting cap covering the top, back, and sides of the head.

25: "some names that end in zee": The editors of the Oeuvres suggest that, read in conjunction with Rimbaud's poem "Devotion," a favorite of Breton, the "zee" names may be Dutch, as in Zuyderzee. We have adopted this reading in translating the line. The "*zée*" (Zeus) is also a genus of yellow, spiny-finned, ocean food-fishes, including the John Dory (*Zeus faber*), sacred in antiquity to Zeus or Jupiter.

"BLACK FOREST" ["FORÊT-NOIRE"]

The asterisk in the title refers to the last line of the poem, indicating that it is spoken by Rimbaud. In 1875 Rimbaud was living in Stuttgart, a city near the Black Forest. The poet Paul Verlaine, recently released from jail, came to visit him. A night of trooping from bar to bar led to a quarrel, then to a fight. In his 1930 note on the poem, Breton mentions the "Rimbaud ... who had just bashed Verlaine on the head in the middle of the Black Forest, and got out of there" (*Oeuvres I,* 1086). This poem may attempt to reproduce Rimbaud's mental state after the altercation.

In the *Surrealist Manifesto* (1924) Breton recalled that in his first poetic experiments he "had been led to concentrate my attention on the more or less partial sentences which, when one is quite alone and on the verge of falling asleep, become perceptible for the mind without its being possible to discover what provoked them." He continues:

> The virtue of the spoken word (and the written word all the more so) seemed to me to derive from the faculty of foreshortening in a striking manner the exposition (since there was exposition) of a small number of facts, poetic or other, of which I made myself the substance. Rimbaud had not proceeded any differently. I was composing, with a concern for variety that deserved better, the final poems of *Mont de piété,* that is, I managed to extract from the blank lines of this book an incredible advantage. These lines were the closed eye to the operations of thought that I believed I was obliged to keep

> hidden from the reader. It was not deceit on my part, but my love of shocking the reader. I had the illusion of a possible complicity, which I had more and more difficulty giving up. I had begun to cherish words excessively for the space they allow around them, for their tangencies with countless other words that I did not utter. The poem "Black Forest" derives precisely from this state of mind. It took me six months to write it, and you may take my word for it that I did not rest a single day (*Manifestoes,* 19–20).

Breton then confesses that he may have been influenced by the vogue of "cubist pseudo-poetry," and admits to entertaining "a sneaking suspicion…that from the viewpoint of poetry I was off on the wrong road…" (*Manifestoes,* 19–20).

1–2: "Out"/ "derby": "Out" appears in English in the text; Rimbaud knew the language, and had spent time in England. The derby or bowler hat is Rimbaud's: "At the beginning of the poem we see him grabbing his hat" (Breton's 1930 note, *Oeuvres I,* 1086).

3: "Saint-Gobain": A town in northern France in the Aisne *département,* the latter being the scene of much of World War I, and the location of a vast forest. Saint-Gobain has made mirrors since the seventeenth century. Whether Breton is here referring to an actual individual or personifying a narcissistic boredom as "Mme. de Saint-Gobain" remains unclear.

10: "*What a wholesome wind*": In *Mad Love* (1937) Breton mentions that this line, from Rimbaud's poem "The Cassis River" (*"La Rivière de cassis"*) had always had a "magic effect" on him (*Mad Love,* 9).

11: "The Author of The Guardian Angel Inn": The author of this tale was Sophie Rostopchine (1799–1894), daughter of Count Rostopchine, governor of Moscow. She became the Countess of Ségur when she married Eugène de Ségur of the distinguished Ségur family. In 1917

Jacques Vaché wrote to his and Breton's mutual friend, Théodore Fraenkel, to thank him for sending a copy of this book. (For Fraenkel, see the note for the dedication of "Rendezvous," below.)

15: "Kepler Hegel": Johannes Kepler (1571–1630), the famous German astronomer who studied at the University of Tübingen. The philosopher Georg Wilhelm Friedrich Hegel (1770–1831) also studied there. Breton was a great admirer of Hegel's thought.

16: "the faithful friend": *Der gute Kamerad* was a poem written by Ludwig Uhland in 1809 and later set to music by Friedrich Silcher in 1825. It became one of the songs of the German armies, used at funeral and memorial services. Is this an ironic reference to Verlaine?:

Once I had a good buddy
I've never found one better
The drum that beat for battle
Drew him right beside me
At the same speed and step

A bullet hurtled toward us
Was it meant for me or him
It tore him to pieces
Then he lay at my feet
As if he were part of me

His hand reached out for mine
But I needed to load my gun
I couldn't grasp your hand
We'll meet again in eternity
Good buddy of mine.

"FOR LAFCADIO" ["POUR LAFCADIO"]

Lafcadio is the central character in André Gide's novel *Les Caves du Vatican* (translated into English as *Lafcadio's Adventures*). The Surrealists were great admirers of the *acte gratuit* (gratuitous act), of which Lafcadio is a practitioner. The editors of the *Oeuvres I* show that this poem, too, is a collage created out of materials borrowed mostly from friends.

2: "MAM": Breton noted in 1930 that "MAM was a somewhat swanky shop at the end of the Avenue de l'Opéra ... and probably the abbreviation of Saint-Mammès, too" (*Oeuvres I*, 1091). The name of the shop probably derives from *"mam'selle,"* the familiar pronunciation of *"mademoiselle."* Breton wrote this poem in 1918 at Saint-Mammès, where he had been transferred to the 81st Heavy Artillery Regiment.

9: Words spoken by "a certain Fraenkel who remembered Ubu Roi a little too much," Breton wrote in another 1930 annotation to the proofs of *Mont de piété*. (See the note to the dedication of "Rendezvous," below.)

10–11: These lines are taken from Rimbaud's *Illuminations* ("Enfance: I").

12: From a letter to Théodore Fraenkel from Jacques Vaché: "My God, it's hot—I'll never be able to win so many wars!!!" (*Oeuvres I*, 1092).

18: "collector of Excise Taxes": The "taxes" were evidently the words "excised" from the letters and conversation of other writers and Breton's friends for use in his own poems. The French is wittier: *"receveur de Contributions Indirectes."*

"MISTER V" ["MONSIEUR V"]

Title: "Mister V" is Paul Valéry, the last of the great *symboliste* poets and an important bridge from symbolism to modernism. He was greatly admired by the young Breton, who sent the older poet drafts of many of the poems in *Mont de piété.* Later, he and Paul Éluard parodied Valéry's *Notes sur la poésie.*

1: Valéry lived near the Place de l'Étoile. The absence of the capital "E" in the poem shows Breton playing with this reference.

13–14: The contemporary poles of literary influence tugging at Breton—Pierre ("Peter") Reverdy and Paul Valéry, and a reference to the old saw of "robbing Peter to pay Paul." When Breton sent Valéry his "For Lafcadio," the older poet threatened never to write to him again if Breton did not send him a "perfect sonnet," ordering: "March! Take it or leave it." Breton wrote to Fraenkel: "I leave it" (*Oeuvres I,* 1095).

15: "find the king": Jean-Pierre Cauvin and Mary Ann Caws note "the custom of passing around the *galette des rois* (Twelfth-Night cake) from which each person takes a piece in the hope of finding the baked-in *fève* (bean), thus becoming *roi de la fève* (king of the bean)" (*Poems,* 243).

"A NOT-VERY-SOLID HOUSE" ["UNE MAISON PEU SOLIDE"]

In his *Lautréamont et nous,* Aragon explicitly stated that this poem was a collage: only the names in a news item taken directly from a newspaper had been changed (*Oeuvres I,* 1097). Apollinaire, admired and befriended by the young Breton, and creator of the word "surrealism," was, in a sense, the "watchman" of the French avant-garde. His untimely death from the Spanish influenza in 1918 (as he recuperated from a head wound sustained in combat) came as a serious blow to the poets and painters who had grouped themselves around him.

p. 11: "Rue des Martyrs": An actual Paris street, and a fitting place-name for a sacrifice.

"THE MYSTERIOUS CORSET" ["LE CORSET MYSTÈRE"]

Another exercise in collage composition, in which Breton has reassembled a variety of newspaper or magazine headlines and pieces of text. Breton printed other examples of these kinds of poems in the *Surrealist Manifesto* (1924): "It is even permissible to entitle POEM what we get from the most random assemblage possible... of headlines and scraps of headlines cut out of the newspapers..." (*Manifestoes*, 41–43). In his 1930 annotations he mentioned "'The Mysterious Corset,' a very beautiful sign that can still be seen on a second floor balcony on the Rue de la Paix" (*Oeuvres I*, 1098).

EARTHLIGHT [CLAIR DE TERRE] (1923)

In her discussion of *Clair de terre* in the *Oeuvres I*, Marguerite Bonnet writes: "After the general crisis of confidence through which Breton passed at the beginning of 1923, a crisis whose acme is marked by the interview given to Roger Vitrac for *Le Journal du Peuple* on April 7 and the decision to stop writing that is affirmed there, a renascence is created by and for his poetry" (*Oeuvres I*, 1183). In addition, see the note for "To Rrose Sélavy," below.

Epigraph: The editors of the *Oeuvres I* were unable to locate the source of this quotation. The title of the collection may have been inspired by lines of Mallarmé's sonnet "*Quand l'ombre menaça de la fatale loi*" / "When the shadow menaced with its fatal law":

> *Oui, je sais qu'au lointain de cette nuit, la Terre*
> *Jette d'un grand éclat l'insolite mystère,*
> *Sous les siècles hideux qui l'obscurcissent moins.*

Yes, I know that the Earth, far off from this night,
Casts the radiant mystery of unprecedented light
Which the hideous centuries can never obscure.

(*Mallarmé,* Weinfield trans., 66; *Oeuvres I,* 1183)

Dedication: Saint-Pol-Roux (real name, Paul Roux, 1861–1940) came to be called "the Magnificent" after he added this paraph to his signature on a literary questionnaire. He early chose to live a life of obscurity in Brittany. His work first saw publication in the *symboliste* period, and he authored many plays and poems. Many of his books and manuscripts were destroyed by the Nazis in 1940. They killed the longtime family servant and raped and shot his daughter. Saint-Pol-Roux died a few days after the attack. The Surrealists had a high regard for his writing, and Breton (who visited him in 1923) called him "The Master of the Image."

"FIVE DREAMS" ["CINQ RÊVES"]

Dedication: Giorgio de Chirico (1888–1978): Italian "metaphysical" painter whose early, mysterious canvasses had a profound impact on dadaism and surrealism. (In the dedication, Breton gives de Chirico's name as "Georges," the French version.)

I

p. 16: "the Grands-Augustins part of town": The northeast corner of the Sixth Arrondissement, bordered by the Quai des Grands-Augustins (at the Seine).

p. 16: The "genius" may be Paul Valéry, who served Breton as an intellectual guide between 1914 and 1920 and helped him in other ways. (*Oeuvres I,* 1192.)

p. 16: Germain Nouveau (1852–1920): Poet, self-styled "Humilis." After a bohemian youth (including a spell in London with Rimbaud), he was influenced by the Verlaine of *Sagesse*, became a devout Roman Catholic, and wrote *Poèmes d'Humilis* (1911). Breton included his work in his *Anthology of Black Humor*, where Breton wrote that "absolute nonconformism regulated this life from start to finish" (*Black Humor*, 160).

p. 16: Jules Barbey d'Aurevilly (1808–1889): Essayist, novelist, critic, and short story writer (including the famous *Les diaboliques*, 1874), he came from a royalist, Catholic family, and managed to balance an extreme Catholicism with an equally extreme *dandyisme*.

p. 17: Georges Gabory: (1899–1978): Poet, novelist, and essayist who worked on various magazines and as a reader for the Gallimard publishing house, author of *Coeurs à prendre* (1921) and *Poésie pour Dames seules* (1922). Clancier groups him with the pre-surrealist "Fantasist" poets, whose ranks included P.J. Toulet, Tristan Derême, Francis Carco, and Pierre Mac Orlan. (*De Rimbaud au Surréalisme*, 234.)

p. 17: Pierre Reverdy: (1889–1960): One of the major twentieth century French poets, whose theories of the poetic image and literary cubism served as an inspiration to Breton.

p. 17: "The light ... ": The repetition of this word is oddly reminiscent of the ending of Ibsen's drama *Ghosts* (1881). At its conclusion the syphilitic young artist, Oswald Alving, mutters "... give me the sun." To his mother's horror he continues to repeat "The sun—the sun," as the curtain falls.

The editors of the *Oeuvres I* mention Goethe's deathbed cry: "More light!" Breton used it to open his statement of January 1937 about the Second Moscow Trials. (See *What Is Surrealism?*, 168–72, for a translation of the text.)

II

p. 17: "the Trocadéro station": A Métro stop on the Right Bank of Paris.

III

p. 19: Roger Lefébure: Paris attorney who represented the poet Tristan Tzara and other dadaists. During the performance of Tzara's play *Le Coeur à barbe (The Bearded Heart)*, Léfebure "handed us—Paul Éluard and myself—over to the police," wrote Breton in *Nadja* (18). This 1923 event marked the definitive break between the dadaists and the surrealists.

p. 19: Paul Poiret (1879–1944): French decorator and fashion designer, close to some of the cubist painters. He introduced cubist-influenced styles in women's clothing around 1908.

p. 19: Paul Éluard (1895–1952): The pen name taken by Eugène Grindel, major surrealist poet and one of the major French poets of the twentieth century. Éluard was a leading Surrealist and comrade of Breton until their split over political differences in 1938.

IV

p. 20: "the Apollo Gallery": A room in the Louvre Museum in Paris. It contains a famous ceiling mural by Delacroix featuring the Greek god Apollo slaying the Python.

p. 20: Adonis: Beloved by Aphrodite, this beautiful youth was killed during a hunt by a boar—or by a jealous Ares or Hephaestus disguised as a boar. Adonis was a divinity of vegetation and fertility whose disappearance marks the harvesting of the crops. (*Oxford Classical Dictionary*, 6–7.)

p. 21: Charles Baron: Poet and brother of the poet Jacques Baron, known among the surrealists "on account of some vague boxing lessons he once took" as "Baron the Boxer." See Aragon's *Paris Peasant* (31).

p. 21: Louis Aragon: (1897–1982): Soon known simply by his last name, he was one of Breton's chief lieutenants in the surrealist movement. Perhaps his most enduring work, in a massive oeuvre that includes poetry and many novels, is *The Paris Peasant (Le Paysan de Paris,* 1926). His political commitment to the French Communist Party led to a break with surrealism in 1930. He is also remembered as a heroic activist and poet of the French Resistance during World War Two. See note to 1.9 of "For Lafcadio" for his photograph.

V

p. 21: Marcel Noll: Contributor to *La Revolution surréaliste,* the surrealist publication, and eventual director of the Surrealist Gallery established in Paris in 1926. Aragon saluted his "enormous capacity to promote confusion" (*The Paris Peasant,* 31). In the *Manifesto of Surrealism* Breton noted him as one who has "performed acts of ABSOLUTE SURREALISM" (*Manifesto,* 26).

p. 22: Philippe Soupault: Poet, novelist, journalist, Soupault (1897–1990) was a member of the surrealist group until 1927. Also one of the dadaists, in collaboration with Breton he wrote *The Magnetic Fields* (1920), the "first Surrealist text."

p. 24: "Nantes": For a time Breton was stationed there during the First World War.

"COUNTERFEIT COIN" ["PIÈCE FAUSSE"]

The French title, *"Pièce fausse,"* literally means a "false piece," but the idiomatic meaning is "counterfeit coin." The poem should probably be read as a chant, or an aria. Its shape on the page suggests the symmetry of the vase described in the first part. Taken together, the title and the form make a visual pun. The poem derives from the last stanza of "Camaïeu," a youthful poem of Breton's. (See *Oeuvres I,* 41–42; 1195.) The text also appears in *Vous m'oublierez (You'll Forget Me),* the dramatic sketch coauthored by Breton and Philippe Soupault in 1920.

Dedication: Benjamin Péret (1899–1959): Major surrealist poet and loyal ally of Breton.

"PST" ["PSTT"]

The title is a pun on the PST, the French abbrevation for the annual telephone directory of the P.T.T. (Postes-Télégraphes-Téléphones) and "pst" or "psst" (spelled "pst" or "pstt" in French), the attention-getting noise. No doubt this is a "found poem," taken right from the Paris telephone directory. Ironically, no entry appears for Breton, André, except for his end signature.

"THE REPTILE HOUSEBURGLARS" ["LES REPTILES CAMBIOLEURS"]

This is the first of a number of poems Breton wrote about pubescent girls in victim roles, including "Unconscious" and *Violette Nozières.*

Dedication: Janine: Janine Kahn (1903–1972), a sister of Simone (Kahn) Breton, married the poet and novelist Raymond Queneau in 1928.

"MAPS ON THE DUNES" ["CARTES SUR LES DUNES"]

Dedication: Giuseppe Ungaretti (1888–1970), the great Italian poet who lived in Paris from 1912–14. Like Breton, he was an early practitioner of unpunctuated free verse. Originally close to the Futurist artists, Ungaretti later founded Hermeticism. Breton was responding to a French poem by the Italian poet which he had dedicated in 1919 "To André Breton / for *Pawnshop.*"

p. 32: "the bugle": A reference to the famous patriotic song by Paul Déroulède (1846–1914), "The Bugle." (*Oeuvres I,* 1198)

"UNBREAKABLE FISHNET" ["ÉPERVIER INCASSABLE"]

Dedication: Gala Éluard (1894–1982) was Elena Dimitrovnia Diakonova. One of the *femmes fatales* of the surrealist circle, she married the poet Paul Éluard in 1917 and later became the wife of Salvador Dalí, who depicted her in many of his most famous paintings.

Title: The French word for "fishnet," "*épervier,*" can also mean "sparrow-hawk." The editors of the *Oeuvres I* suggest that the phrase may have come from a poem by Jules Romains, "*La conscience qui devient*" / ["The consciousness to come"] from his volume *La vie unanime* (1901): "The breaths [...] / That shape the unbreakable fishnet of love / Where captive beings tremble pell-mell [...] (Romains, 208).

"MEMOIRS OF A HIGHWAY STOCK CERTIFICATE." ["MÉMOIRES D'UN EXTRAIT DES ACTIONS DE CHEMINS."]

Another collage poem, this time using portions of newspaper or magazine headlines of various sizes.

The editors of the *Oeuvres* note: "We can mentally complete the text, '*chemins de fer*' ["railroads"] and believe that the failure to complete the formula and the emptiness of the allusion to the world of

finance (*actions* = "stocks") serves to reject the reality of everything that pertains to the world of getting and spending" (1199). Like "Isle," the editors conclude that this text serves as an *illustration,* especially because of the absence of pagination. The "completed" text could then be translated: "Memoirs of a railroad stock certificate."

Stocks are not sold for highways, of course, but Breton's insistent punctuation mark allows, perhaps, for the reading of the poem that we have adopted. The lack of closure noted in the *Oeuvres* might also result in a translation like "Memoirs of a stock certificate for rail."—but this solution seems awkward.

"THAT'S PRISON TOO" ["C'EST AUSSI LA BAGNE"]

In the original edition of *Earthlight* (1923) this poem appeared as the eighth section of "*Le Volubilis et je sais l'hypoténuse*" ["The Morning Glory and I Know the Hypotenuse"], a phrase uttered by Robert Desnos in a state of hypnotic sleep in 1922 while Breton was present. He originally dedicated the entire poem to his wife, Simone.

Dedication: Francis Picabia (1879–1953) was a Dadaist painter and poet, close to the Surrealists in their early days. He and Breton worked together on Dadaist events before Breton formed the Surrealist group.

"RENDEZVOUS" ["RENDEZ-VOUS"]

Dedication: Théodore Fraenkel (1896–1964): Physician and a long-time friend of Breton; they attended the Collège Chaptal and medical school together. Robert Desnos remembered Fraenkel "talking like Père Ubu," the Alfred Jarry creation, and called him "the most human incarnation of Dada, notably refusing to write or publish anything at all" (*Nouvelles Hebrides,* 329–330). Fraenkel introduced Breton to the woman who would become his first wife, Simone Kahn.

p. 36: "the Vandal Prince": The Vandals were a Germanic people who maintained a kingdom in North Africa from 429 to 534 A.D. They sacked Rome in 455.

p. 36: "bombyx": The scientific name for the silkworm moth.

"THERE'S NO WAY OUT OF HERE" ["IL N'Y A PAS À SORTIR DE LÀ"]

10: "Atlantes": Atlantes (the plural form of "Atlas") are male (and sometimes female) figures used as supports for an entablature, a balcony, or other architectural projection, especially when such figures are posed as though they were actually upholding great weights, like Atlas carrying the world.

19: "An artillery lieutenant": Breton was attached to an artillery unit during World War I. However, here he may be referring to his friend Apollinaire, who did reach the rank of lieutenant in the artillery before being wounded.

30: *The Raft of the Medusa*: The masterpiece of the French artist Théodore Géricault. This painting, which hangs in the Louvre, was finished in 1819. It graphically portrays the contemporary shipwreck off the west coast of Africa of the *Medusa*. The painting caused a scandal when it was exhibited, partly because of its hellish details. After the French naval frigate ran aground on July 5, 1816, at least 147 people were set adrift on a hurriedly constructed raft; all but fifteen died in the thirteen days before their rescue, and those who survived endured starvation, dehydration, and cannibalism.

"BLOTTER OF ASH" ["LE BUVARD DE CENDRE"]

Dedication: Robert Desnos. See "My Death by Robert Desnos" for a note on this poet.

4: "borage": A blue-flowered, hairy-leaved plant used in salads. It is derived from an Arabic word meaning "father of sweat," from its use as a diaphoretic.

11: The Vaucluse: A district in Provence, for the most part very rural.

"IN THE EYES OF THE GODS" ["AU REGARD DES DIVINITÉS]

12: "reseda": A flower notable for the urn-shaped horned capsule at its tip; also, a grayish green color. It exudes a powerful and pleasant odor.

23: "the white Fathers": Possibly priests of the Benedictine order, whose garb is completely white.

"EVERY PARADISE ISN'T LOST" ["TOUT PARADIS N'EST PAS PERDU"]

Dedication: Man Ray (1890–1976) was the only American in the original surrealist group. He was a pioneer in photography and filmmaking as well as a painter and sculptor.

1: "weathercocks": The *coq de roche* is also a bird called the cock-of-the-rock. Found in the Amazon valley, it is about the size of a pigeon, with orange-colored plumage, a pronounced crest, and orange-red flesh. It builds its nest on rock. We have chosen the weatherbird because of the storm imagery in the poem.

"MY DEATH BY ROBERT DESNOS" ["MA MORT PAR ROBERT DESNOS"]

Title: Robert Desnos (1900–1945): Breton characterized Desnos, one of surrealism's enduring poets, in his 1928 work *Nadja* as a writer who "continues seeing what I do not see, what I see only after he shows it to me" (*Nadja,* 31). In 1930 Breton attacked Desnos for his "un-Surrealist" activities as a journalist. Desnos coauthored a bitter response called *Un cadavre (A Corpse).*

A 1922 painting by Desnos called *Death of André Breton* was shown in the exhibition mounted by Patrick Waldberg called *Surrealism 1922–1942* at the Musée des Arts Décoratifs in Paris (1972). Two other paintings by Desnos, one called *Here Lies Éluard,* and another, *Death of Max Morise* (both dated 1923) were also displayed. Marguerite Bonnet has stated that there is no direct relation between the picture and the Breton poem. (*Oeuvres I,* 1207).

"My Death…" is laced with the imagery of Roman Catholicism. The last line evokes the traditional symbol for the feminine, a circle with a cross beneath it.

1: "academicians…": This line may refer to a time in the mid-1920s when Desnos worked as a medical research writer.

11: *The Thinker*: Probably the well-known sculpture by Auguste Rodin.

13: "Trinity's topmost height": Perhaps a reference to the Paris church of that name on the Rue Saint-Lazare in the Opéra (9th Arrondissement). It stands not far from the notorious former red-light district in Pigalle.

"CHOOSE LIFE" ["PLUTÔT LA VIE"]

34: "Pont-à-Mousson": An industrial town on the Moselle River near Nancy. One of its chief products are the manhole covers—stamped "Pont-à-Mousson"—found in the streets of Paris.

"SILHOUETTE OF STRAW" ["SILHOUETTE DE PAILLE"]

Dedication: Max Ernst (1881–1976): German painter, sculptor, and collage artist, Ernst was one of the best-known of the dadaists and surrealists. Breton, on his honeymoon, met him in Cologne in 1921. Ernst moved to Paris in 1922 and soon joined the surrealist group.

26: "the cuttlefish": A sea mollusk related to the squid. Some species squirt out a black inky fluid when attacked.

"ISLAND" ["ILE"]

Another typographical poem. Here, Breton has inverted the "I"—or has found it that way in a French newspaper or magazine—for an odd visual effect. The type appears to have come from the logo of *Le Figaro,* the French newspaper. (See the note to "Memoirs...," above.

"IN THE VALLEY OF THE WORLD" ["DANS LA VALLÉE DU MONDE"]

Dedication: Joseph Delteil (1894–1978) was a French poet and novelist who enjoyed a great success in the 1920s, during part of which time he was embraced by the surrealist group. His novels include *Sur le fleuve Amour* (1923), *Choléra* (1923), and *Jeanne d'Arc* (1925). Breton had broken with him as early as July of 1925, when an exchange of letters appeared in *La Révolution surréaliste.* "Between ourselves," Breton wrote, "your Joan of Arc is a vast heap of rubbish...

The question should be of finding out whether you are a swine or an ass (or a swine and an ass)" (Jean, 148–49). After publishing three more novels, Delteil left Paris in 1930 for the Languedoc, where he became a winegrower. He published his autobiography, *La Deltheil-lerie,* in 1968.

12: "lanceolate leaves": A type of leaf shaped like a lance tip, e.g., birch leaves. Both ends of the leaf are pointed.

34: "heliotropism": The tendency to move or bend in response to sunlight.

"A THOUSAND THOUSAND TIMES" ["MILLE ET MILLE FOIS"]

1: "mysterious symbols eleven in number": This appears to be a personal mythology invented by Breton, most likely the adaptation of an occult philosophy. The symbols are reminiscent of the ten *sefiroth* or divine emanations in the Jewish *Kabalah* ("the symbols hide the mind from me"). Breton's symbols also suggest the twelve signs of the zodiac. Or they may simply derive from the eleven letters in Breton's name.

25: "the doubly ogival buckler": A buckler was a small round shield that was held in the hand or worn on the arm. The phrase "doubly ogival" suggests the shape of the vaulted ceilings in Gothic churches, crisscrossed by ribs called "ogives."

"THE EGRET" ["L'AIGRETTE"]

Title: Egret: A heron with plumage of long white feathers. As "aigrette"—another possible title for this poem—it can mean a spray of feathers from this bird as well as a spray of gems worn in a woman's hat or hair, something Breton could have seen at the Paris Opera House. The complexity of Breton's associations is further indicated

by two additional meanings of the word. "Aigrette" can also signify the featherlike cluster of rays that emanate from the sun's corona during a total eclipse, as well as the sharp point attached to an electrical conductor (a lightning rod, for example) to facilitate the formation of a corona discharge. The title in itself serves as a miniature object-lesson in Breton's exploitation of the surrealist properties inherent in language.

2–3: "breasts / Composed... the ornamental letter to begin the word amour": In typography an ornamental letter depicts the word that it begins. The rounded shape of the "a" suggests the form of the female breast.

Our thanks to Professor Roy Breunig for this observation.

12: "the Tree of Heaven": The ginkgo (or maidenhair) tree, grown since ancient times around temples in China, where it is considered a sacred plant.

16: "the Arc de Triomphe du Carrousel": Not the famous Arc de Triomphe located in the Place Charles de Gaulle, but another triumphal arch in the gardens of the Louvre in Paris.

18: "the Legislature": The French phrase "*les Chambres*" indicated the two houses of the French parliament, comprised of the Chamber of Deputies and the Senate at the time this poem was written. The *Chambre des députés* is located in a classical building overlooking the Seine and facing the Place de la Concorde.

"BROKEN LINE" ["LIGNE BRISÉE"]

Dedication: Raymond Roussel (1877–1933): Enormously wealthy poet, dramatist, and novelist (*Locus Solus, Impressions of Africa*) whose idiosyncratic methods of composition led to the creation of works highly esteemed by the surrealist group.

17: "patience plants": Patience is an herb (*Rumex Patientia*) formerly used in salads.

26: "the Sisters of Charity": An uncloistered order of nuns active in teaching and nursing.

"SUNFLOWER" ["TOURNESOL"]

See sections 3 and 4 of *Mad Love* for Breton's own reading of this poem, which for him prefigured the meeting with Jacqueline Lamba, his second wife.

1: "Les Halles": A district in the First Arrondissement in Paris which once centered around a wholesale food market, now demolished. The other streets and landmarks mentioned in the poem are not far from this site.

3: "arums": An arum is a kind of tuberous herb. It is a poisonous plant.

7: "the Chien Qui Fume": A night spot in Les Halles—"the Smoking Dog," as in cigarette-smoking.

12: "the Ball of the Innocents": Innocents' Day is a festival celebrated by the Roman Church on December 28 in memory of the massacre of the children by Herod. It was one of the series of days known as the Feast of Fools. The day is still observed as a feast day and merry-making for children in Catholic countries, and particularly as an occasion for practical joking. It was also considered an unlucky day.

15: "Rue Gît-le-Coeur": Literally, "Here-Lies-the-Heart Street."

29: "Étienne Marcel": Marcel (1316–1358) was a clothier who led an early revolt against the French monarchy. He was assassinated in 1358.

"THE SUN ON A LEASH" ["LE SOLEIL EN LAISSE"]

1: "The big white cold storage room": In September of 1923, Simone Breton wrote to her sister, Denise Kahn, that she and André found themselves on the terrace of a café in the port at Lorient, where her husband "is writing very beautiful poems." "The big cold storage room of white stone," she noted, "big as a fortress, ruthlessly cuts off the view of the western coast," and immediately referred to the beginning of this poem (*Oeuvres I,* 1214–15).

14: "torpedo fish": An actual fish, flat like a ray, that uses an electric shock to stun its prey.

22–25: See the note to line 1, above, for the setting of the poem.

"TO RROSE SÉLAVY" ["À RROSE SÉLAVY"]

Title: Rrose Sélavy ("Eros, c'est la vie"—"Eros, that's life") was the name of Marcel Duchamp's self-proclaimed feminine alter ego, for whom he created puns ("My niece is cold because my knees are cold.") and even mock advertisements. Robert Desnos appropriated Rrose for a long sequence of elaborate puns that appeared in his first major collection, *Corps et biens* (1926).

Epigraph: The epigraph cites the headline of an interview with Breton by Roger Vitrac ("*André Breton n'ecrira plus*") that appeared in the *Journal du Peuple,* April 7, 1923. In it Breton asserted that he, as well as Paul Éluard and Robert Desnos, "had the intention of writing only a little bit of the time from now on." This stance was part of Breton's attempt to "ruin literature" (*Oeuvres I,* 1214–1215).

FREE UNION [L'UNION LIBRE] (1931)

This is probably the most famous and widely-translated surrealist poem. The French suggests the English phrase "living together," but the poem has been translated too many times as "Free Union" to change the title now.

A number of translators have given the phrase "*Ma femme*" (with which most lines of the poem begin) as "My wife." The title and what we know of the poem's inspiration seem to rule out such a rendering.

Breton originally published "*L'Union libre*" anonymously as a separate book in 1931. According to critic Marcel Jean, editor of *The Autobiography of Surrealism,* the poem was inspired by Breton's affair with Suzanne Muzard, for whom he divorced his first wife, Simone Kahn. Suzanne supplied her own reflections on her "passage in the surrealism of the years 1927–32" in Jean's anthology (190–92). To the contrary, José Pierre in *Oeuvres II* insists that neither Suzanne Muzard, with whom Breton had parted company several months before he drafted the poem in May of 1931, nor Marcelle Ferry (another lover), nor his wives Jacqueline or Elisa (both of whom he met years later, and to whom he referenced the poem in dedications and letters) inspired "Free Union," but that the poem constitutes an "homage to woman in general" (*Oeuvres II*, 1318).

The tradition behind this poem is the *blazon,* a form invented by French poet Clément Marot (1596–1544).

Hope Glidden writes in a note to a translation of a Marot *blazon:*

> The *blazon* is a descriptive poem that praises (or mocks) one body part detached from the whole (the eyebrow, the teeth, the cheek, the ear, the hair, and so on. Thanks to Marot's initiative, the genre reached its

high point in the *Blasons anatomiques du corps feminin,* and the great poets of the age... competed with one another to write examples that were witty and often bizarre. *Lyrics of the French Renaissance: Marot, Du Bellay, Ronsard.* English versions by Norman R. Shapiro. Introduction by Hope Glidden. Notes by Norman R. Shapiro and Hope Glidden (Chicago and London: The University of Chicago Press, 2002/2006), 98–101.

Breton extends his *blazon* to include the entire body of the woman that he praises. See Shakepeare's Sonnet 130 ("My mistress' eyes are nothing like the sun") for another example of the *blazon.*

5: rosette: *Rosette* is the French diminutive of *rose.* It may refer to a small flower design; hence, various flower-shaped or rotational symmetric forms. In botany, a rosette is a circular arrangement of leaves, with all the leaves at a similar height. Though rosettes usually sit near the soil, their structure is an example of a modified stem.

8: "stabbed eucharist tongue": "In *Nadja* the kiss is compared to communion; Breton notes how one of these 'petrifying coincidences' that heightens the work is the arrival next day at his home of a detail from *The Profanation of the Host* by Uccello. The stabbed host is a malefic rite evoked by Huysmans, particularly in *Là-bas,* chapter XX" (*Oeuvres II,* 1341). See *Nadja* (93–94). But this note is curious. In the Uccello painting, one of six altar panels on this theme (and also known as *The Miracle of the Desecration of the Host*), the eucharist is not stabbed but burned. There is at least one painting (not by Uccello) that shows the host being stabbed, yet another example of the anti-Semitism of the period.

12: "edge of a swallow's nest": Perhaps Breton is referring to the materials that hang down from the bottom of some swallow nests.

20: "marten": A meat-eating mammal similar to a weasel. Martens are trapped for their fur.

21: "Midsummer Night": The night of June 24, near the summer solstice. Traditionally in Europe, Midsummer Night is a time of revelry and celebration, as in Shakespeare's *A Midsummer Night's Dream.* The French name for it, *la nuit de Saint-Jean,* stems from the fact that June 24 is Saint John's Day in the Roman Catholic calendar.

22: "angelfish nest": The angelfish is a tropical fish commonly found in home aquariums.

22: "privet": A privet is a flowering plant in the genus *Ligustrum.* The genus contains about 50 species of erect, deciduous or evergreen shrubs, sometimes forming small or medium-sized trees, native to Europe, North Africa, Asia and Australasia.

29: "weaverbirds": The lightweight build, strong feet and pointed bill of the village weaver enable it to hang adroitly while threading the first grass strips of its nest.

31: "Val-d'or": Literally, "Valley of Gold." A place-name, most likely. There is a Val-d'Or in Québec, Canada, but Breton didn't visit Québec until long after he had published *L'Union Libre.*

51: "gladiolus": Gladiolus (from Latin, the diminutive of *gladius,* a sword) is a genus of perennial cormous flowering plants in the iris family (Iridaceae).

52: "placer": A deposit of valuable metals formed by the winnowing action of a swiftly flowing stream.

52: "platypus": An Australian mammal, furry and with a duck-like bill. Unlike most mammals, its young are hatched from eggs.

THE REVOLVER WITH WHITE HAIR [LE REVOLVER À CHEVEUX BLANCS] (1932)

Title: Anna Balakian, in her 1971 study *André Breton: Magus of Surrealism,* sees connections between poems in this book and Breton's studies of the occult. Her book is permeated with comments and analyses of what she calls Breton's "hermeticism." Balakian's volume is an excellent place to begin the study of Breton's engagement with the occult arts.

"ONCE UPON A TIME TO COME" ["IL Y AURA UNE FOIS"]

p. 69: "Huysmans": Joris-Karl Huysmans (1848–1907) was a French novelist who produced both naturalistic and Symbolist work. *En rade* (*Stranded* and *Becalmed* are used as different translations of the title), published in 1887, was a naturalistic tale, but one in which, according to J.H. Matthews in *Surrealism and the Novel,* the author "accomplishes enough to exert a powerful attraction over the surrealists":

> In Jacques Marles [the novel's hero], tortured by the world of reality and obliged in his search for release from its oppressive presence to retire into dreams, is prefigured the surrealist artist, for whom day-to-day reality is no more than the projection of a frustrating universe which, in separating man from his desires, fills him with inescapable anguish. The sufferings of Marles foreshadow the pessimistic conclusions about life from which surrealism took its impetus in its exploration of possible paths to another reality, promising experiences the real world denies us. In Marles's reaction against reality is to be seen the very instinct from which surrealism draws strength. (Matthews, 38)

Marles and his wife take up residence in the deserted Château des Lourps outside Paris, where they "hope to seek a shelter, a roadstead [*rade*, also translated as "harbor"], where they could drop anchor and take council together...." Like Breton, who doesn't have the money to create his ideal retreat in "Once Upon a Time to Come," Marles is a man "dismayed, defenseless against the money worries that froze the packing in his brain and threw it back brutally into the inextricable entanglement of real life." His release "is imaged in his rambling exploration of the château," in which "reality is shown to be crumbling..." (Matthews, 33–34). As he focuses his attention on minute details of the real world about him, Marles moves into a sequence of dreams in which Huysmans "uses naturalism to discredit reality [and] to lend credence to the imaginary" (Matthews, 36). Breton, of course, seizes the bull by the horns and creates his own "château."

p. 70: "Saint Anthony's nights": Saint Anthony of Egypt lived in the third and fourth centuries. He was known for his elaborate visions of the devil, who was said to tempt the saint in many different guises. Anthony's visions are the subject of a famous painting by Salvador Dalí as well as works by Hieronymous Bosch and Matthias Grünewald, and a novel by Gustave Flaubert.

p. 70: "But where are the snows of tomorrow?": A play on one of the most famous lines of French poetry, "But where are the snows of yesteryear?" (*Mais où sont les neiges d'antan*), written by Francois Villon (b. 1431) in his *Testament*.

p. 72: "Merovingian chairs": The Merovingian period in European art spans the fifth through the eighth centuries A.D. The house that Breton describes in the second part of this text is reminiscent of the unusual castle that appears in the *Surrealist Manifesto* (1924).

p. 73: "Luna Park": A famous, extravagantly lighted attraction during the heyday of New York City's great amusement park, Coney Island.

"THE PINK DEATH" ["LA MORT ROSE"]

25: "the adonis": A flower commonly known as pheasant's eye, having golden or blood-red blossoms, "as if from the blood of Adonis" (*A Latin Dictionary*).

38: "the angelica": A genus of herbal plants used in perfumes, oils, and liqueurs. Its flowers can be white or purple.

"NO INDICTMENT" ["NON-LIEU"]

Published the year before the Nazis came to power in Germany, this poem may be a response to the growing fascist movement that would soon engulf Europe.

7: "the ibis": A wading bird native to warm climates and sacred to the Egyptians. In the Tarot deck, the ibis symbolizes Thought. Both the ibis and the pool (representing Universal Consciousness) appear in the Tarot card called the Star, number 17 in the Major Arcana. This card provided the title for Breton's book *Arcanum 17* (*Arcane 17*, published in 1944).

"ON THE ROAD THAT GOES UP AND DOWN" ["SUR LA ROUTE QUI MONTE ET DESCEND"]

26: "Chateau-Ausone": A red wine from the Saint-Émillion region of France (near Bordeaux). The name derives from the estates of the Roman poet Ausonius (ca. 310–395), who was born in Bordeaux. After the murder of Gratian, whom he had educated at the imperial court in Rome, and who had elevated him to the consulship, Ausonius returned to his estates and their large vineyards.

34: "the mirrors of Venice": This could mean the reflection of Venice in the canals or the lagoon.

"GHOSTLY STANCES" ["LES ATTITUDES SPECTRALES"]

67: "Banyans banyans": The banyan is a tree native to southern Asia that can grow to cover an enormous area. Its branches send aerial roots back down into the soil. It is a tree considered sacred throughout India.

"SPARKS HOTEL" ["HÔTEL DES ETINCELLES"]

18: "the diabolo": A game in which an hourglass-shaped top is balanced and spun on a string stretched between the tips of two sticks. The top is also called a diabolo, derived from the toy's trademark name.

"THE FOREST IN THE AXE" ["LA FORÊT DANS LA HACHE"]

p. 94: "so they'll come back to life": Perhaps a reference to *Locus Solus* (1914), Raymond Roussel's novel (presented on the stage in 1922) in which the dead are revived with drugs called vitalium and resurrectine. See also "Curtain Curtain": "The freedom to bring back to life the beings that I missed" (26).

p. 94: "The Italian straw hat": The name of a famous play by Eugène Labiche. Dating from 1851, this farce concerns the misadventures of a young bridegroom trying to replace a straw hat eaten by a pony.

"ALL THE SCHOOLGIRLS TOGETHER" ["TOUTES LES ÉCOLIÈRES ENSEMBLE"]

The last two lines of this poem contain a complex pun. The actual phrase in the dictation was *Le coeur m'en dit,* meaning "I had a notion, whim." The phrase was heard incorrectly as *Le coeur mendie,* which means: "My heart pleads."

"KNOT OF MIRRORS" ["NOEUD DES MIROIRS"]

24: "the Emperor Maximilian's lonely execution": Ferdinand Maximilian Joseph (1832–1867) was an Austrian archduke who was placed on the throne of Mexico by Napoléon III, the French emperor. Overthrown by Benito Juárez, Maximilian was executed by Mexican forces on a hill outside the town of Querétaro, northwest of Mexico City, on June 18, 1867. Édouard Manet did a series of works based on this event.

16–21: According to Cauvin and Caws, this is the pharmaceutical formula for the treatment of angina pectoris. "Gallop rhythm" ("*le bruit de galop*") is a medical term that describes an abnormal heart rhythm marked by the occurrence of three distinct sounds in each heartbeat, like the sound of a galloping horse.

26: "the sundial's *style*": An unusual meaning of the word "style," defined as "the projecting piece on a sundial that shows the time by its shadow." (*Concise Oxford Dictionary*)

"A MAN AND A WOMAN COMPLETELY WHITE" ["UN HOMME ET UNE FEMME ABSOLUMENT BLANCS"]

3–4: In *Nadja* (published four years earlier than *The Revolver...*) Breton noted "the charm of naked walls with their flowered papers and their shadows of mantlepieces, in apartment houses under demolition..." (*Nadja,* 108).

"CHEVAL THE MAILMAN" ["FACTEUR CHEVAL"]

This poem pays homage to Joseph Ferdinand Cheval (1836–1924), a mailman who collected stones and shells along his route and used them to build his "Ideal Palace" in his home town of Hauterives in France. The Palace is an ornate temple adorned with sculptures of an-

imals and monsters, a true masterpiece of "naive art" comparable to Simon Rodia's handcrafted towers in Los Angeles. Cheval had no artistic training. A book detailing his life and work, *Le Palais Idéal du Facteur Cheval,* was published in 1981.

23: "Vaucanson ducks": Jacques de Vaucanson (1709–1782) was the inventor of the mechanized silk loom, an important breakthrough of the Industrial Revolution. Before his commercial inventions he made automated figures, the most successful of which was a toy duck, built in 1739. The duck could drink, eat, defecate, and move like a real bird.

"THE VERTEBRAL SPHINX" ["LE SPHINX VERTÉBRAL"]

7: "arums": The arum is an herb with heart-shaped leaves found in Europe and Asia.

15: "vetiver": A light grayish olive color. Also, an aromatic grass (called "khuskhus") whose fragrant roots yield an oil used in the manufacture of perfume. The grass is also woven into mats in tropical India.

24: "Prince Rupert's Drop": A congealed blob formed by dropping hot glass into water. It resembles a tadpole with a long tail. The globule explodes violently when the "tail" is scratched or a piece broken off. The device is named after the nephew of Charles I of England, who brought several of them to the king as presents. The king turned them over to the Royal Society, which explored their properties. See a very entertaining video about the Drop at http://www.youtube.com/watch?v=xe-f4gokRBs.

"VIGILANCE" ["VIGILANCE"]

1: "the Saint-Jacques Tower": Long ago part of the church called Saint-Jacques-de-la-Boucherie that was pillaged during the French Revolution, this Gothic tower now stands alone in a square on the

Right Bank near the Paris City Hall in the 4th arrondissement. The church was constructed in the early 1500s. Breton attributed occult powers to it, and wrote of it in *Mad Love* and *Arcanum 17*. The alchemist Nicolas Flamel was buried under the church floor.

17: Note the spiky, bone-like projections from each top corner of the structure.

"UNCONSCIOUS" ["SANS CONNAISSANCE"]

This poem appears to have been based on a real incident. It prefigures *Violette Nozières,* which also concerns a young woman awakening to her sexuality, and violation.

11–12: "Rue Saint-Martin / Gate of the same name": The Saint-Martin district, where this poem is set, is on the Right Bank of Paris, not far from the Place de la République. In the 1930s, when this poem was written, it was a working-class neighborhood.

15: "Euphorbia": A large genus of plants from which the family Euphorbiaceae takes its name. The Euphorbiaceae also contain a milky juice, or latex, used to manufacture rubber. Many of the species are poisonous, but others give tapioca, castor oil, commercial oils, resin, fruits, and medicines.

26: See the first note to p. 94.

"LAST MAIL PICKUP" ["DERNIÈRE LEVEE"]

6: Place Blanche: The Café Cyrano, in the Place Blanche, was an early surrealist meeting-place. (Bancquart, 8)

"THE DEADLY HELPING HAND" ["LE GRAND SECOURS MEURTRIER"]

Title: Marguerite Bonnet notes that "even the title, 'Le Grand Secours meurtrier,' of the poem in which Lautréamont has the central place, in *The Revolver with White Hair*, refers to the history of the convulsionaries of Saint-Médard who, during their trances, begged onlookers for the corporal punishments that were called "big" [*grand*] or "small" [*petit*] helping hands [*secours*], according to their severity." "These 'helping hands' consisted of blows with a stick, punches, various brutalities that could lead to crucifixion." They were called "deadly... when the use of a sword was called for. To refuse these helping hands would be to expose the convulsionaries to death. Those who administered them were called 'helpers' or 'convulsionists.'" The Saint-Médard cemetery was attached to the Saint-Medard church in Paris where the convulsionaries performed their rites, centered on the tomb of Deacon Jean de Pâris, where alleged miraculous cures took place. (See note to 1.18, below.)

A book about one episode of the convulsionary phenomenon published in 1788 was found in Breton's library. It contained a chapter entitled "Beginning of convulsions subject to the big helping hand [*grand secours*]" (*Oeuvres II*, 1346–7).

Louis Basile Carré de Montgeron, author of *La vérité des miracles de M. de Pâris démontrée contre M. l'Archevêque de Sens,* 3 tomes, 1737, 1741 et 1747, experienced a conversion at Deacon Pâris' tomb and undertook to write a history of what he witnessed, including the activities of the convulsionaries.

See the superb account of the convulsionaries given in Chapter 2, "The Convulsionists," in *The Dark Side of Enlightenment: Wizards, Alchemists, and Spiritual Seekers in the Age of Reason* by John V. Fleming (New York London: W. W. Norton & Co., 2013), 73–104. Fleming recommends "the single most comprehensive book on the episode," *Miracles, Convulsions, and Ecclesiastical Politics in Early Eighteenth-Century Paris* by B. Robert Kreiser (Princeton: Princeton University Press, 1978).

1: "Lautréamont": Isidore Ducasse (1846–70) wrote under the pseudonym Le Comte de Lautréamont. Virtually unknown in his time, Lautréamont was later hailed by the surrealists for the imagery and iconoclasm of his work.

3: "The 'pedestal of quinine pills' can give rise to a reminiscence: the double statue of the chemists Pelletier (1788–1842) and Caventou (1795–1858)—who in 1823 isolated quinine from the bark of the cinchona tree—stood on a raised pedestal situated at the crossroads of Boulevard Saint-Michel and Auguste-Comte and l'Abbé-de-l'Épée streets; these bronze figures, melted down during the Occupation, are today replaced by a commemorative pedestal, much more modest than the first. Breton, who during the years 1918–1920 had been familiar with these spots, was able to see looming up before his eyes this impressive pedestal to support his imaginary statue" (*Oeuvres II,* 1347).

4: "the author of the Poems is lying flat on his stomach": Lautréamont published a volume with this title in 1870. "Hermaphroditos, son of Hermes and Aphrodite, had rejected the advances of the nymph Salmacis. Unable to resign herself to this rejection, Salmacis persuaded Zeus to merge their two bodies forever, hence the strange union producing one bisexed being with male sexual organs and the voluptuous curves of a woman. Stretched out in erotic abandon on the mattress provided by [the sculptor] Bernini, the figure sleeps. Yet Hermaphroditos has only fallen half asleep: the twisting pose of the body and the tension apparent down to the slightly raised left foot are indicative of a dream state" (Louvre website).

"It is likely that Breton here mingles the memory of the Hellenistic statue of which a Roman copy figures in the Musée du Louvre, *Hermaphrodite endormi [The Sleeping Hermaphrodite],* that depicts the sleeper lying flat on his stomach, the one of strophe 7 of the second of the *Chants of Maldoror,* dedicated to the sleep of the hermaphrodite" (*Oeuvres II,* 1347–48).

In *Maldoror* Lautréamont employs the following refrain: "Over there in a grove surrounded by flowers slumbers the hermaphrodite, sound asleep upon the sward, drenched with his tears" (*Maldoror,* Lykiard trans., 47.) It is not impossible that both Isidore Ducasse and André Breton meditated on the same statue in the Louvre.

10: "The swan of Montevideo": Lautréamont was born and raised by French parents in Montevideo, Uruguay. In Chant 6, strophe 6 of *Maldoror,* he transforms himself into a black swan:

> Arrived in sight of the lake, he sees it thronged with swans. He thinks it a safe retreat; with the help of a metamorphosis, without abandoning his burden, he mingles with the other birds of the bevy. Behold the hand of Providence where one was tempted to believe it absent, and profit by the miracle I am about to relate you. Black as a crow's wing, thrice he swam among the knot of dazzlingly white palmipeds; thrice he kept that distinctive hue which made him resemble a lump of coal. It was because God in His justice would not permit his guile to deceive even a bevy of swans" (*Maldoror,* Lykiard trans., 197).

18: "convulsionaries": See note to the title of this poem.

VIOLETTE NOZIÈRES (1933)

In 1933 the eighteen-year-old Violette Nozière, a high school student, poisoned her father and mother; the father died, but the mother survived to prosecute her daughter for the crime, which attracted great attention in France. (Janet Flanner, writing as "Genêt" in *The New Yorker,* gave the episode extensive coverage stateside.) The surrealists' addition of a final "s" to the name is an error.

The scandal became a *cause célèbre* for the surrealist group, which believed Violette's accusations of incest ("Sometimes my father forgets that I am his daughter," the young woman told the judge, a line that Breton used in his poem) and saw her "protest" as a triumph of the imagination over petit bourgeois morality. The group produced a collective pamphlet, called *Violette Nozières* (Brussels, 1933), with poems contributed by Paul Éluard, E.L.T. Mesens, Breton, Benjamin Péret, and artwork by Dalí, Ernst, and others. In 1963, after years of imprisonment, Violette was pronounced "rehabilitated" by the Court at Rouen and pardoned for her crime. She married, raised a family, eventually joined a nunnery, and died in 1968.

Violette Nozière by Jean-Marie Fitère (Paris: Presses de la Cité, 1975), served as the basis for Claude Chabrol's 1978 film, released in English-speaking countries as *Violette.* A recent study was written by Sarah Maza: *Violette Nozière: A Story of Murder in 1930s Paris* (Berkeley Los Angeles London: University of California Press, 2011).

35: The word "*viol*"—the first four letters of Violette's name—means "rape" in French.

67: "*L'Action Française*": The newspaper of a neo-Fascist political group of the same name.

75: "Champ-de-Mars": The formal garden under the Eiffel Tower in Paris.

THE AIR OF THE WATER [L'AIR DE L'EAU] (1934)

"WORLD IN A KISS" ["MONDE DANS UN BAISER"]

3: "lion monkeys": Any of several South American marmosets having tufted tails and well-marked neck ruffs of long hair.

6: "axolotls": Any of several larval salamanders of the genus Ambystoma found in the mountain lakes of Mexico and the western U.S. "Axolotl" is a Nahuatl word, a combination of *atl* (water) and *xolotl* (doll or toy).

14: egrets: An egret is a bird that is any of several herons, most of which are white or buff, and several of which develop fine plumes (usually milky white) during the breeding season.

21: "coreopsis": A genus of herbs (family Compositae), many of which are used in cultivation and which have showy flower heads. The plural (also "coreopsis") is a plant of the genus *Coreopsis*, commonly known as tickseed.

"THE TELESCOPE-FISH CRACKS STONES" ["LE POISSON-TÉLESCOPE"]

1: "telescope fish": A goldfish of a breed characterized by a very short thick body, a large and double tail fin, and protuberant eyes. The celestial telescope is a kind of goldfish in which the eye pupils are directed upward.

11: "stag beetle's horns": The stag beetle bears long and often branched mandibles suggesting the antlers of a stag.

17: "Iceland spar": A transparent calcite, the best of which is obtained in Iceland. It easily cleaves into rhombohedrons, and is used for polariscope prisms because of its strong double refraction. Also known as Iceland crystal and white calcite.

"THE SEXUAL EAGLE EXULTS" ["L'AIGLE SEXUEL EXULTE"]

9: "eye-agate": An old oriental gem made by cutting an agate so that it resembles an eye. Also known as the aleppo stone, since it was used as a remedy for Aleppo boils.

"THE MARQUIS DE SADE HAS GONE BACK" ["LE MARQUIS DE SADE A REGAGNÉ"]

1: The Marquis de Sade—Donatien-Alphonse-François de Sade (1740–1814)—authored many texts which were considered obscene by the French government as latc as 1957. His criminal debaucheries led to a death sentence, which was commuted to life imprisonment, mainly in the Bastille. He was freed by the Revolution. Later, when a pamphlet of his offended Napoleon, he was confined to the lunatic asylum at Charenton. De Sade was a hero to the surrealists, and the *Dictionnaire abrégé du surréalisme* (1938), cited Petrus Borel, Guillaume Apollinaire, and Maurice Heine in his favor.

"IN THE BEAUTIFUL HALF-LIGHT OF 1934" ["AU BEAU DEMI-JOUR"]

20: "radiolarians": The radiolaria (from the late Latin, *radiolus*—"small sunbeam") comprise a large order of rhizopods.

"ZINNIA-RED EYES OF THE TOO WHITE" ["YEUX ZINZOLINS"]

The translators offer their thanks to Professor Leroy Breunig, who invented the phrase "zinnia-red eyes."

3: "Jacqueline X": Jacqueline Lamba, Breton's second wife, whom he met and married in 1934, no doubt served as the inspiration for this suite of love poems. In her study of Breton, Anna Balakian published the translation of a letter from Jacqueline to her that described the genesis of the poem:

> *L'Air de l'eau* was written very shortly after my meeting with André in about one week, which he spent in the outskirts of Paris, at the edge of a little river. I don't remember the name of the place, but he knew it well and loved it, and knew that it was propitious to him... This poem is entirely about me, or better about us; he went off by himself, circumstances having prevented me from following him, at that moment. I think, however, that it is clearer to say that he preferred being alone to write it just as he stopped suddenly in our walk across Paris the night of the "Tournesol," detaching himself as if better to note what was true.... After having written *L'Air de l'eau* he came back and read it to me, making a commentary of it, explaining each sentence. But later I have heard him say that he had all sorts of reservations about analysis of what did not become immediately evident in his own poems, as one cannot autoanalyze oneself completely. It must also be remembered that automatic writing was over for him at that period and although always spontaneously born, each sentence was worked over, endlessly, as a thing that is foreseen and at the same time outlived" (Balakian, 143).

However, Cauvin and Caws note: "Intriguing in this context is the letter *X*, by which Breton designates at the end of *Nadja* a woman with whom he had a liaison after separating from Simone, his first wife, and before his encounter with the 'scandalously beautiful' Jacqueline" (*Poems*, 250). Might X have been Suzanne Muzard, the possible muse of *Free Union*?

"IT WAS GOING ON FIVE IN THE MORNING" ["IL ALLAIT ÊTRE"]

18: "Undine": A water nymph, an elemental spirit of the water (from the Latin *unda*—"wave"). Also, the title of a fairy tale by the German novelist and dramatist Friedrich Freiherr de la Motte Fouqué (1777–1843), "a poignant presentation of the popular story of the water sprite who marries a mortal—a theme which offered obvious possibilities to a Romantic mind steeped in the antithesis of the real and supernatural" (Thorlby, 278). *Undine* was later made the subject of an opera by E.T.A. Hoffman (1813), for which Fouqué himself compiled the libretto. The name is also spelled "Ondine."

In his biography of Breton, Mark Polizzotti offers this information:

> A day or two before he was to leave for Brussels, at seven-thirty on May 29, Breton was holding the afternoon meeting [of the Surrealist group] at the Place Blanche when a woman with brilliant blonde hair entered and immediately seized his attention. He later described her entrance:
>
>> She was very young, but her distinctive youth did not strike me at first sight, because of this illusion she gave of moving about, in broad daylight, within the gleam of a lamp. I had already seen her here two or three times, her coming announced before I saw her each time by an undefinable quiver moving from one pair of shoulders to the next, from the door of this café toward me. For me this motion itself... has always, whether in art or in life, signaled the presence of the *beautiful.* And I can certainly say that here, on the twenty-ninth of May 1934, this woman was

> *scandalously* beautiful.... From the first moments, a quite vague intuition had encouraged me to imagine that the fate of that young woman could some day, no matter how tentatively, be entwined with mine.

Breton was all the more struck by his "intuition" in that, in the previous weeks, he had reexamined the question of "preordained" or "fortuitous" encounters in a new essay, focusing on a particular incident that he had witnessed while lunching at the Maison Bergey bistro near his apartment: he had been musing about the pretty waitress when he boss sharply summoned, "Here, Ondine!" [*Ici, l'Ondine!*]. "The exquisite and childish answer came in a whisper, perfect," Breton wrote: "Ah, yes, one dines here!" [*Ah! oui, on le fait ici, l'Ondine!*] Could there be a more touching scene?" Ever watchful for marvelous coincidences, he now became convinced that the charming "Ondine" had foreshadowed the arrival of the "*scandalously* beautiful" blonde in the Café de la Place Blanche. (Polizzotti, 360–1)

When she met Breton, Jacqueline was studying painting and "making her living as a nude underwater dancer at a large Montmartre music hall.... It was after her evening's performance that she was to meet Breton" (Polizzotti, 362).

"AND AGAIN MOTION" ["ET MOUVEMENT"]

3: "tapas": Plural of the Marquesan and Tahitian word *tapa*. The bark of the paper mulberry or of an Hawaiian tree *(Pipturus albidus)*. Also, the tapa cloth is a coarse cloth made in the Pacific islands from the pounded bark of the paper mulberry, breadfruit, and other plants, usually decorated with geometric patterns.

33: *L'Humanité*: A newspaper founded by French socialist leaders Jean Juarès (1859–1914) and Aristide Briand (1862–1932), which became the daily organ of the Socialist Party in France.

34: "the Oirat": An autonomous administrative division of the Russian S.F.S.R., created in 1932, within the Siberian area. The Oirat is entirely rural, mountainous, and the climate severe. Russian colonization of the Oirat began in the nineteenth century, and fifty per cent of the population is Russian.

"IF I WERE YOU I'D WATCH OUT" ["A TA PLACE JE ME MÉFIERAIS"]

2/7: In *Orlando Furioso* (1516), Ludovico Ariosto's romantic epic, Ruggiero sees the naked Angelica chained to a rock on the Isle of Tears as he flies on his winged hippogriff. She is to be fed to an orc, a giant sea-monster. After the beast has been subdued,

> The hippogriff, responding to the spur,
> Braces its hoofs and rises in the air;
> Away Ruggiero pillion carries her,
> Depriving thus the monster of its fare.

Orlando Furioso, Reynolds translation; Canto X.112.1–4.

21: "Danaë": "Acrisius, who was married to Aganippe, had no sons, but only this one daughter Danaë whom Proteus (Acrisius' brother) had seduced; and, when he asked an oracle how to procure a male heir, was told: 'you will have no sons, and your grandson must kill you.' To forestall this fate, Acrisius imprisoned Danaë in a dungeon with brazen doors, guarded by savage dogs; but, despite these precautions, Zeus came upon her in a shower of gold, and she bore him a son named Perseus." Robert Graves, *The Greek Myths,* I.238.

"THEY TELL ME THE BEACHES" ["ON ME DIT QUE LÀ-BAS"]

1–4: A description of Tenerife, the largest of the Canary Islands. Its famous Pico de Teide occupies nearly two-thirds of the entire island. In 1706 an immense quantity of lava poured from the peak, flowing to the sea and nearly filling the harbor of Garachico. Other large flows of lava occurred in 1795 and 1798.

See *Mad Love* (section 5) for the "black sand" that so fascinated Breton.

"ALWAYS FOR THE FIRST TIME" ["TOUJOURS POUR LA PREMIÈRE FOIS"]

16: "Grasse": Located to the north of Cannes, Grasse is particularly celebrated for its perfumery. Oranges and roses are cultivated abundantly in the neighborhood.

31: "Rue Notre-Dame-de-Lorette": Found at the heart of north central Paris, this street is a major thoroughfare of the 9th Arrondissement (Opéra). The Catholic church, for which the street is named, stands at the intersection of the Rue Notre-Dame-de-Lorette and Rue St. Lazare. In common parlance *une lorette* signified a "woman of easy virtue," a sobriquet that derives from what was the red-light district in which the church stands. The Church itself is named for the "Holy House" in Loretto, Italy, on the Adriatic, which overshadowed all other centers of pilgrimage by the fifteenth century.

IN THE BLACK LAUNDRY SHED *[AU LAVOIR NOIR]* (1936)

In the Black Laundry Shed is penetrated by references to Aeschylus' *Prometheus Bound*. There are the butterflies, analogous to the winged Chorus of the play; handcuffs reminiscent of Prometheus' chains; the isolation of the narrator ("I had been left alone for a long time," 147);

and the thunderbolts that carry out Zeus' continuing punishment of the recalcitrant Titan. The phrase "you are in your fate" (148) summarizes Prometheus' dilemma, pinioned to a cliff in the waste land of the Caucasus for bringing fire (intelligence) to mankind.

In the last section of the text these references become explicit: "You're motionless, chained to the cold rock above the cliff..." (148). But the line attributed to the Chorus is actually delivered by Io herself at the end of her entrance speech in the Aeschylus play. (See notes for pp. 148–49.) Breton's identification with the persecuted female, here Io, is a theme found throughout his work.

p. 145: "Anything can appear in a hailstone, the Virgin can appear to children, that's been seen...": On May 26, 1907, six days after the local town council of Remiremont had banned the traditional parade honoring the Virgin Mary, hailstones the size of tomatoes floated down like snowflakes, without shattering. According to an ecclesiastical investigation, 107 citizens saw stones that bore the distinct image of Mary and the Christ Child in twenty different locations throughout the town. (In protest, citizens had struck a medallion modeled after a local statue of the Virgin said to contain miraculous properties.) The Archdeacon Vuillemin noted that the sworn reports "were, on the whole, of a remarkable precision. It was not a vague form that the witnesses saw, but an absolutely clear effigy, corresponding in every detail with the medal struck in memory of the statue" (Rogo, 141–158).

p. 146: "the wings of the female blue": The blue constitute a group of small butterflies of the Lycaenidae family. The females have bright blue wings, darker than the males.

p. 147: "death's-head moth": A very large European hawk moth, so called from a figure resembling a human skull on the back of the thorax.

p. 148: "the Ice Palace": Then a famous skating rink in Paris.

p. 148: "the stinging fire that goads her on": Hera discovered Zeus' infidelity with Io, after which the Lord of the Gods transformed his paramour into a cow. Hera sent a gadfly to sting her and chase her all over the world.

p. 149: "dominoes": Here "domino" means a small mask covering the top part of the face, worn at costume balls. The French is *loup,* which also means "wolf."

p. 149: "Argus": Hera claimed Io after her transformation and ordered the shepherd Argus, whose body was covered with eyes, to guard her. Hermes, dispatched by Zeus to retrieve Io, killed him. Hera moved his eyes to the feathers of peacocks.

BIBLIOGRAPHY

Aragon. *Paris Peasant.* Translated from the French by Simon Watson Taylor. (London: Jonathan Cape Ltd., 1971; Pan Books/Picador, 1980).

Ariosto, Ludovico. *Orlando Furioso 1.* Translated with an Introduction by Barbara Reynolds. (Harmondsworth and Baltimore: Penguin Books, 1975).

Balakian, Anna. *André Breton: Magus of Surrealism.* (New York: Oxford University Press, 1971).

Bancquart, Marie-Claire. *Paris des Surréalistes.* (Paris: Seghers l'archipel edition, 1971).

Benedikt, Michael. *The Poetry of Surrealism: An Anthology.* With Introduction, Critical Notes and New Translations by Michael Benedikt. (Boston–Toronto: Little, Brown and Company, 1974).

Breton, André. *André Breton: Selections.* Edited by Mark Polizzotti; (Berkeley: University of California Press, 2003).

______________. *Arcanum 17.* Translated from the French by Zack Rogow; (Los Angeles: Green Integer, 2004).

______________. *Nadja.* Translated from the French by Richard Howard. (New York and London: Grove Press/Evergreen Books, 1960).

______________. *Manifestoes of Surrealism*. Translated from the French by Richard Seaver and Helen R. Lane (Ann Arbor: University of Michigan Press, 1969).

______________. *Mad Love*. Translated from the French by Mary Ann Caws. (Lincoln and London: University of Nebraska Press, 1987).

______________. *Anthology of Black Humor.* Translated from the French and with an Introduction by Mark Polizzotti (San Francisco: City Lights Books, 1997).

______________. *Oeuvres complètes: I*. Édition établie par Marguerite Bonnet avec, pour ce volume, la collaboration de Philippe Bernier, Étienne-Alain Hubert et José Pierre. (Paris: Gallimard NRF, Bibliothéque de la Pléiade, 1988).

______________. *Oeuvres complètes: II*. Édition établie par Marguerite Bonnet avec, pour ce volume, la collaboration de Philippe Bernier, Étienne-Alain Hubert et José Pierre. (Paris: Gallimard NRF, Bibliothéque de la Pléiade, 1992).

______________. *Poems of André Breton: A Bilingual Anthology.* Translated and edited by Jean-Pierre Cauvin and Mary Ann Caws. (Austin: University of Texas Press, 1982; reprinted Boston: Black Widow Press, 2006).

______________. *What Is Surrealism?: Selected Writings*. Edited and Introduced by Franklin Rosemont. (New York: Monad Press / Pathfinder Press, 1978).

______________. *Young Cherry Trees Secured Against Hares [Jeunes cerisiers guaranti contre les lièvres]*. Cover design by Marcel Duchamp. Translated by Edouard Roditi (New York: View Editions, 1947; reprinted Ann Arbor: University of Michigan Press, Ann Arbor Paperbacks, 1969).

______________. *Selected Poems.* Translated by Kenneth White (London: Jonathan Cape, Grossman Publishers/Cape Editions, 1969).

Clancier, Georges-Emmanuel. *De Rimbaud au Surréalisme: Panorama critique.* (Paris: Pierre Seghers Éditeur, 1953).

Desnos, Robert. *Nouvelles Hebrides et autres textes 1922–1930.* Édition établie, présentée et annotée par Marie-Claire Dumas. (Paris: Gallimard NRF, 1978).

Fitère, Jean-Marie. *Violette Nozière.* (Paris: Presses de la Cité, 1975).

Flanner, Janet. *Paris Was Yesterday (1925–1939).* Edited by Irving Drutman (New York: Popular Library, 1970).

Graves, Robert. *The Greek Myths, Volumes I and II.* (Baltimore: Penguin Books, 1955).

Ibsen, Henrik. *Four Great Plays.* Translated by R. Farquharson Sharp. With an Introduction and Prefaces to each Play by John Gassner. (New York: Bantam Books, 1958).

Jean, Marcel, ed. *The Autobiography of Surrealism.* (New York: Viking Press, The Documents of 20th-Century Art series, 1980).

Jouve, Jean-Pierre, Claude Prévost, Clovis Prévost. *Le Palais idéal du Facteur Cheval: Quand le songe devient la réalité.* Paris: Éditions du Moniteur, 1981).

Lautréamont, Comte de / Isidore Ducasse. *Lautréamont's Maldoror* Translated by Alexis Lykiard. New York: Thomas Y. Crowell Company, Apollo Editions, 1970/1972).

Mallarmé, Stéphane. *Collected Poems.* Translated and with a Commentary by Henry Weinfield. (Berkeley Los Angeles London: University of California Press, 1994).

Matthews, J.H. *Surrealism and the Novel.* (Ann Arbor: University of Michigan Press, 1966).

Maza, Sarah. *Violette Nozière: A Story of Murder in 1930s Paris.* (Berkeley Los Angeles London: University of California Press, 2011).
Polizzotti, Mark. *Revolution of the Mind: The Life of André Breton.* revised and updated edition. (Boston, Mass.: Black Widow Press, 2009. Originally published by Farrar, Straus, and Giroux, New York, 1995).

Reid, Joyce M.H. *Concise Oxford Dictionary of French Literature.* (U.S.A.: Oxford University Press, 1986).

Reverdy, Pierre. *Le Gant de crin: notes.* (Paris: Flammarion, Éditeur, 1927; 1968).

Rimbaud, [Arthur]. *Illuminations.* Translated with a Preface by John Ashbery. (New York and London: W. W. Norton, 2011).

Rogo, D. Scott. *Miracles: A Parascientific Inquiry into Wondrous Phenomena.* (New York: The Dial Press, 1982).

Romains, Jules. *La vie unanime: poème.* (Paris: Mercure de France, 1913).

Shapiro, Norman R., translator. *Lyrics of the French Renaissance: Marot, Du Bellay, Ronsard.* Introduction by Hope Glidden. Notes by Norman R. Shapiro and Hope Glidden (Chicago and London: The University of Chicago Press, 2002/2006).

Thorlby, Anthony, ed. *European Literature: The Penguin Companion to Literature 2.* (Baltimore: Penguin Books, 1969).

•

The Oxford Classical Dictionary. Edited by M. Cary, J. D. Denniston, J. Wight Duff, A. D. Nock, W. D. Ross, H. H. Scullard. With the assistance of H. J. Rose, H. P. Harvey, A. Souter. (London: Oxford at the Clarendon Press, March 1949; reprinted 1961).

A Latin Dictionary, Founded on Andrews' edition of Freund's Latin dictionary revised, enlarged, and in great part rewritten by Charlton T. Lewis, Ph.D. and Charles Short, LL.D. (Oxford: Clarendon Press, 1879).

The Concise Oxford Dictionary. Tenth Edition. Edited by Judy Pearsall (New York: Oxford University Press, 1999).

ZACK ROGOW's translations include *Arcanum 17* by André Breton. He is the cotranslator of *Shipwrecked on a Traffic Island and Other Previously Untranslated Gems* by Colette, published by State University of New York Press. Rogow's English version of Colette's novel *Green Wheat* was published by Sarabande Books and nominated for the PEN/Book-of-the-Month Club Translation Award and for the Northern California Book Award in translation. His translation/adaptation of Marcel Pagnol's play *Marius* was produced by the Storm Theatre in New York and by the Aurora Theatre in Berkeley. He received a Bay Area Book Reviewers Award (BABRA) for his translation of George Sand's novel, *Horace*. Rogow served as editor and artistic director for two volumes of *TWO LINES: World Writing in Translation* and is currently a contributing editor at *Catamaran Literary Reader.* He teaches in the low-residency MFA in writing at the University of Alaska Anchorage. **www.zackrogow.com**

BILL ZAVATSKY has translated *The Poems of A. O. Barnabooth* by Valery Larbaud with Ron Padgett (Black Widow Press), Robert Desnos' first book (in *Tether* magazine), *10 Poems* by Arthur Rimbaud (Omerta), Ramón Gómez de la Serna's *greguerías,* and other works. His books of poems are *Theories of Rain and Other Poems* (SUN), *Where X Marks the Spot* (Hanging Loose Press), and *Haiku & Co.* (Omerta). Poems have recently appeared in *upstreet* and *Catamaran* and in the anthologies *The Face of Poetry* (University of California Press) and *Up Late: American Poetry Since 1970* (Thunder's Mouth). Bill's poems have appeared as liner notes on CDs by jazz pianists Bill Evans and Marc Copland. He taught high school for many years in New York City, at the University of Texas (Austin), and at the Eugene Lang College of the New School University. He has reccived fellowships in poetry from the New York State Council on the Arts, the National Endowment for the Arts, the MacDowell Colony, and the John Simon Guggenheim Foundation. Currently Bill leads a poetry workshop at the Morningside Heights Branch of the New York Public Library in Manhattan.

TITLES FROM BLACK WIDOW PRESS

TRANSLATION SERIES

A Life of Poems, Poems of a Life by Anna de Noailles. Translated by Norman R. Shapiro. Introduction by Catherine Perry.

Approximate Man and Other Writings by Tristan Tzara. Translated and edited by Mary Ann Caws.

Art Poétique by Guillevic. Translated by Maureen Smith.

The Big Game by Benjamin Péret. Translated with an introduction by Marilyn Kallet.

Boris Vian Invents Boris Vian: A Boris Vian Reader. Edited and translated by Julia Older.

Capital of Pain by Paul Eluard. Translated by Mary Ann Caws, Patricia Terry, and Nancy Kline.

Chanson Dada: Selected Poems by Tristan Tzara. Translated with an introduction and essay by Lee Harwood.

Creole Echoes: The Francophone Poetry of Nineteenth-Century Louisiana. Translated by Norman R. Shapiro. Introduction and notes by M. Lynn Weiss.

Earthlight (Clair de Terre) by André Breton. Translated by Bill Zavatsky and Zack Rogrow. (New and revised edition.)

Essential Poems and Writings of Joyce Mansour: A Bilingual Anthology. Translated with an introduction by Serge Gavronsky.

Essential Poems and Prose of Jules Laforgue. Translated and edited by Patricia Terry.

Essential Poems and Writings of Robert Desnos: A Bilingual Anthology. Edited with an introduction and essay by Mary Ann Caws.

EyeSeas (Les Ziaux) by Raymond Queneau. Translated with an introduction by Daniela Hurezanu and Stephen Kessler.

Fables in a Modern Key by Pierre Coran. Edited and translated by Norman R. Shapiro. Full-color illustrations by Olga Pastuchiv.

Forbidden Pleasures: New Selected Poems 1924–1949 by Luis Cernuda. Translated by Stephen Kessler.

Furor and Mystery & Other Writings by René Char. Edited and translated by Mary Ann Caws and Nancy Kline.

The Gentle Genius of Cécile Périn: Selected Poems (1906–1956). Edited and translated by Norman R. Shapiro.

Guarding the Air: Selected Poems of Gunnar Harding. Translated and edited by Roger Greenwald.

The Inventor of Love & Other Writings by Gherasim Luca. Translated by Julian & Laura Semilian. Introduction by Andrei Codrescu. Essay by Petre Răileanu.

Jules Supervielle: Selected Prose and Poetry. Translated by Nancy Kline & Patricia Terry.

La Fontaine's Bawdy by Jean de La Fontaine. Translated with an introduction by Norman R. Shapiro.

Last Love Poems of Paul Eluard. Translated with an introduction by Marilyn Kallet.

Love, Poetry (L'amour la poésie) by Paul Eluard. Translated with an essay by Stuart Kendall.

Pierre Reverdy: Poems, Early to Late. Translated by Mary Ann Caws and Patricia Terry.

Poems of André Breton: A Bilingual Anthology. Translated with essays by Jean-Pierre Cauvin and Mary Ann Caws.

Poems of A.O. Barnabooth by Valery Larbaud. Translated by Ron Padgett and Bill Zavatsky.

Poems of Consummation by Vicente Aleixandre. Translated by Stephen Kessler.

Préversities: A Jacques Prévert Sampler. Translated and edited by Norman R. Shapiro.

The Sea and Other Poems by Guillevic. Translated by Patricia Terry. Introduction by Monique Chefdor.

To Speak, to Tell You? Poems by Sabine Sicaud. Translated by Norman R. Shapiro. Introduction and notes by Odile Ayral-Clause.

MODERN POETRY SERIES

ABC of Translation by Willis Barnstone

An Alchemist with One Eye on Fire by Clayton Eshleman

An American Unconscious by Mebane Robertson

Anticline by Clayton Eshleman

Archaic Design by Clayton Eshleman

Backscatter: New and Selected Poems by John Olson

Barzakh (Poems 2000–2012) by Pierre Joris

The Caveat Onus by Dave Brinks

City Without People: The Katrina Poems by Niyi Osundare

Clayton Eshleman/The Essential Poetry: 1960–2015

Concealments and Caprichos by Jerome Rothenberg

Crusader-Woman by Ruxandra Cesereanu. Translated by Adam J. Sorkin. Introduction by Andrei Codrescu.

Curdled Skulls: Poems of Bernard Bador. Translated by Bernard Bador with Clayton Eshleman.

Disenchanted City (La ville désenchantée) by Chantal Bizzini. Translated by J. Bradford Anderson, Darren Jackson, and Marilyn Kallet.

Endure: Poems by Bei Dao. Translated by Clayton Eshleman and Lucas Klein.

Exile Is My Trade: A Habib Tengour Reader. Translated by Pierre Joris.

Eye of Witness: A Jerome Rothenberg Reader. Edited with commentaries by Heriberto Yepez & Jerome Rothenberg.

Fire Exit by Robert Kelly

Forgiven Submarine by Ruxandra Cesereanu and Andrei Codrescu

Fractal Song by Jerry W. Ward, Jr.

from stone this running by Heller Levinson

Grindstone of Rapport: A Clayton Eshleman Reader

The Hexagon by Robert Kelly

Larynx Galaxy by John Olson

The Love That Moves Me by Marilyn Kallet

Memory Wing by Bill Lavender

Packing Light: New and Selected Poems by Marilyn Kallet

The Present Tense of the World: Poems 2000–2009 by Amina Saïd. Translated with an introduction by Marilyn Hacker.

The Price of Experience by Clayton Eshleman

The Secret Brain: Selected Poems 1995–2012 by Dave Brinks

Signal from Draco: New and Selected Poems by Mebane Robertson

Soraya (Sonnets) by Anis Shivani

Wrack Lariat by Heller Levinson

Forthcoming Modern Poetry Titles

Dada Budapest by John Olson

Fables of Town & Country by Pierre Coran. Translated by Norman R. Shapiro.

Funny Way of Staying Alive by Willis Barnstone

Geometry of Sound by Dave Brinks

Memory by Bernadette Mayer

Penetralia by Clayton Eshleman

LITERARY THEORY / BIOGRAPHY SERIES

Barbaric Vast & Wild: A Gathering of Outside and Subterranean Poetry (Poems for the Millennium, vol. 5). Eds: Jerome Rothenberg and John Bloomberg-Rissman

Clayton Eshleman: The Whole Art by Stuart Kendall

Revolution of the Mind: The Life of André Breton by Mark Polizzotti

ANDRÉ BRETON (1896–1966) was the founder and leader of the surrealist movement. A prolific author, he wrote poetry, the novel *Nadja,* and many books of surrealist thought and criticism, including *Manifestos of Surrealism.* Often considered the central theorist and voice of the movement, Breton was also a dazzling poet. He began his professional life as a medical student, but after World War I soon joined the avant-garde in Paris in the 1920s that reshaped art and much of radical politics. Originally a member of dadaist circles, Breton broke away to form the surrealist group and went on to influence artists and writers globally.